THE MERRY
BRONHILL

THE MERRY
BRONHILL

METHUEN HAYNES

First published in 1987 by
Methuen Haynes
(an imprint of Methuen Australia Pty Ltd)
44-50 Waterloo Road, North Ryde 2113 NSW

National Library of Australia
Cataloguing-in-Publication data

Bronhill, June, 1929-
  The merry Bronhill.

  Bibliography
  Includes index.
  ISBN 0 454 01343 4.

  1. Bronhill, June, 1929-   . 2. Opera – Biography.
  3. Singers – Biography. 4. Women singers – Australia –
  Biography. I. Title.

782.1'092'4

Typeset by Midland Typsetters
Printed by Globe Press

Contents

Preface

For years everyone has been at me to put pen to paper and write my 'book'. For years I've said, 'Yes, OK. One day I will.' Well, at long last it's happened, thanks to Methuen Haynes! About a year ago, Susan Haynes wrote to me and said that if I should ever think of putting down my memoirs, they would be very interested in publishing them. So, if you do happen to enjoy what follows, don't thank me, thank her! Sue offered me a ghost writer, but I said, no, I thought it should come straight from the horse's mouth.

I'm also no good at remembering everything in chronological order, I must be honest. I've never kept a diary as such – even my work diary at times is a mess. Only I know where I'm working, for whom I'm working and what I'm getting! Therefore, I decided that I'd just do the book in chapters about various things that have happened over the years, which means you can pick it up and open it at any chapter and not have to worry about what went before. Does that make sense? Hope so. Sometimes I might sound as though I'm blowing my own trumpet a bit, but I promise you I'm not. I always say, to quote a line from Ivor Novello's *The Dancing Years,* 'No one can tell me when I'm singing well or badly. I know!'

My thanks to all you dears who have been at me for years to 'put it down'. My thanks to Methuen Haynes for forcing the issue. My special thanks, also, to Cathryn Game, who has so wonderfully edited all that I put down. And my thanks to my dear friend Freddie who has been a great help and a tower of strength.

I hope you enjoy it!

June Bronhill

Foreword

I first met June Bronhill in 1968; she was playing the lead role in Ivor Novello's *The Dancing Years* and I was a twenty-year-old stage-hand. I have seen June give many glittering performances in the years since then, but for me *The Dancing Years* will always hold a special magic. I never tired of standing there in the wings watching this incredible woman at such close quarters and feeling a pride that, be it ever so small, I was in some way part of this piece of theatrical magic.

However, it wasn't until years later, 1976 in fact, that I began to know June intimately and to see the private woman, the mother, the crossword addict, the shy, reluctant star. 'What!' I hear you all cry. 'Shy?' Yes, shy! When she is not performing June very rarely goes out, her circle of friends is small, and her pleasures are simple. The movements of the 'social set' don't interest her and I am sure that at times this may give the impression that she is aloof and unapproachable. This is far from the truth. I have suffered many a shopping expedition (that should have taken an hour at most) that has turned into a three-hour epic merely because June always has time to chat with anyone who wishes to engage her in conversation.

Over the past ten years I have watched, listened to and admired the artistry of this little lady; I have shared with her the adulation of the public, but, I think, more importantly, I have shared the other side of Bronhill, the side few ever see. There have been times of bitter disappointment when someone she trusted has let her down badly, the awful realisation that she has been used or 'taken for a ride' by unscrupulous managements; to quote Maria Callas (who also had her share of ups and down), 'Art is not all beauty—for the most part it is a shop'. June has quite often been a commodity in that shop and been sold very cheaply.

There are those times when frustration and insecurity come to the surface of every performer's character, and June is no exception. She can be a prize bitch and there have been times when I could cheerfully have strangled her. I'm sure she's felt the same about me.

One particular incident which comes immediately to mind is the fate of an unsuspecting public relations officer who was lecturing June in a crowded restaurant as to how she should handle a press conference on the following day.

June interrupted. 'May I just say something before you continue?'

'Of course, Miss Bronhill,' said the chap.

'I AM NOT A FUCKWIT!' replied the diva. 'I have had a little to do with the press before!'

The poor man was beside himself and slunk away to a corner, but he need not have done so as June is as quick to forgive and forget as she is to chide. She is also very quick to apologise when she knows she's in the wrong.

This autobiography is in every way the real Bronhill. The words are her own; the photographs she has chosen with care, and the content has been carefully and thoughtfully weeded of anything that may inadvertently hurt those innocent people who are of necessity involved in some of the incidents related in the book.

This is a book written by a great lady who has, to parody Kipling, 'walked with kings, but never lost the common touch'.

I love the book, and I know you will, too.

Rex Wrennall (Freddie!)

1

George and Daisy

It is amazing that we know quite a lot about our parents but so little about their parents and their ancestors. I never knew my grandparents either on my mother's or on my father's side. My sisters and brother knew Grandfather Hall, my mother's father, but none of us knew our father's parents because they lived in England. Why are we often so lazy, not worrying about tracing our lineage? I really can't tell you very much about Mum and Dad's early life, so I'll just tell you the things I remember about them.

Mum was born on 11 August 1895 in Broken Hill. She had two sisters, my Auntie Lil and Auntie Vera, and two brothers, Uncle Harry and Uncle Cecil. I knew that part of my family when I was a child, but I didn't catch up with members of my father's family until I went to England in 1952. Mum was a lovely, ordinary, everyday mother. She worked very hard because she had seven children, five of whom survived, to be looked after. What I remember of Mum is that she seemed to be forever washing and ironing, cooking and cleaning, although we kids did help quite a bit with the house cleaning. Sundays were baking days and she would bake like there was no tomorrow. There would always be about three or four different sponge cakes; the ones that flopped were turned into lamingtons – they were cut into big squares, dipped in chocolate and rolled in coconut. There would be a great big marble cake with lovely marble icing on top; there would be all sorts of scones and something similar to scones called coffee rolls; rock cakes, butterfly cakes; you name it, Mum made it. No wonder I ended up a porky little thing because every Sunday night at tea-time I made sure I had some of everything!

1

Her cooking was fantastic. Apart from all the cakes, she made the most marvellous roast dinners, and wonderful Irish stews, delicious cornish pasties, shepherd's pies, cottage pies. My mouth waters at the thought. Never a night went by without sweets. Mum would make delicious treacle puddings and apricot puddings with home-made custard, none of that stuff out of packets. There were many rolly-pollies and — oh, I could go on and on! On Saturdays in winter, we'd all go to the football in the afternoon and when we came home there would be delicious pancakes for tea, piles of pancakes with all sorts of wonderful fillings. I don't think I ever saw Mum eat one; she was too busy ladling them out for us.

We were always spotlessly clean. Mum didn't have a washing-machine in those days, just the old copper and the hand mangle. She boiled up everything in the copper, sheets, towels, the lot. We used to help her if we were at home. I used to help her with the mangling and iron the hankies, dozens of them! In the very early days Mum ironed with the old flat iron, heated up on the wood stove which would be blazing away even in the heat of summer. There was no such thing as an ironing board, just a couple of blankets and an old sheet on the kitchen table. Everything was immaculately done.

We kids took all this effort for granted, we just accepted it all.

Mum had the sweetest nature imaginable. Her wedding photo shows that she was a pretty, dainty soul. I think when she married she was probably about four foot eleven, much the same as I am now, but as she got older she shrank a little, as so many of us do. Just before she died I used to tower over her.

When Dad worked at the Broken Hill Hospital he would often ask some of the nurses from out of town to have tea with us on Sundays. Sometimes we had as many as fifteen people sitting around our tea table on a Sunday. Then, sure as eggs were eggs, Dad would suddenly look at Mum and say, 'Easy to see we've got company, Daisy, you've got the table napkins out.' This was his way of sending her up, and she would bite every time. 'Oh, George, don't be dreadful. You know we always have table napkins,' she would say.

One day Dad got her an electric iron, which she found the most incredible new-fangled thing. Even when Dad bought her an electric washing-maching, she preferred to boil up the old copper and she never did give up her old mangle. When our refrigerator arrived, Mum was quite taken aback by it and thought it was the most marvellous thing she had ever seen. However, she wouldn't give up the old ice box and the ice man still arrived twice a week with ice. Nor would she part with the water bags. They were hessian bags which you filled with water and hung in the back verandah. The breeze would cool the water. We always had lovely cool drinking water provided by our water bags. The next thing Dad got Mum was an electric stove, but she refused to use it for cake baking. She said, 'Oh, no, George, it's just not the same. The cakes don't turn out the same.' So even in the heat of summer in Broken Hill—and sometimes we would have a heatwave for weeks on end, with temperatures of 110°F (that's 40°C) in the shade—Mum would bake with the old wood stove. We could never talk her out of it.

I've always said that I got my voice from my father, but Auntie Vera told me that I also got my voice from Mum. Auntie Vera said my mother had a very sweet voice when she was young, but I never heard her sing myself. She was probably far too busy!

★

My father, George, was quite a character. He was born on 23 February 1892 in Essex. At the ripe old age of fourteen he got consent from his mother to go to sea. So in 1906 he joined the King Line Ltd. For the first year his pay was £5, £8 in the second year, £12 in the third year and, on the satisfactory completion of his apprenticeship, he would receive a bonus of £10. When he finished his apprenticeship, the Master of the SS *King David*, Henry Fenwick, wrote, 'George F. Gough has served his three-year apprenticeship under my command and has given every satisfaction. He is strictly sober, diligent and most attentive to his duties and I can safely recommend him as a trustworthy young man.'

After about five years at sea, George landed in Australia. It appears that he went into the outback and worked for about a year on stations, learning a lot about the country he would make his home. In 1912 he found his way to Broken Hill. Soon he met Daisy Hall, whom he married in 1915. He had only been in Broken Hill for a short while before he joined the mines and worked underground as an engine driver.

It is a great worry for any family to have a husband, father, brother or son working underground. People in mining communities the world over know that horrible feeling of hearing that siren go to announce that there's been a mine disaster and wondering whether one of yours is involved. As a child I heard the siren going on a few occasions. There is also an unbelievable smell of sulphur associated with a cave-in. Everybody either ran to the mines and stood waiting, or waited at home by the radio for news of what had happened.

My father became a great union man and was one of the people in Broken Hill who helped set up the lead bonus, whereby mine workers shared the profits of the mines, particularly those who worked underground and ran the risk of lead poisoning. When I was about seventeen young men could earn between £70 and £90 a week on the mines. It was wonderful money but they earned it. Another thing that the unions introduced in those days was the idea that the mines were for the Broken Hillites, as we call ourselves. Nobody could just come in from anywhere in Australia and take advantage of the money to be made in the mines. They had to work in another job in Broken Hill for six months before they could apply for work in the mines.

My father was a great man for looking after the workers. He was a great labour man in the days when there were no — or very few — strikes and the labour bosses really looked after the ordinary working man. Naturally, over the years he gained a very good name in the Broken Hill community for being the type of person who would always be a champion of the people. In his early years in Broken Hill he was also on the council and an alderman for three years. Then, in 1932, he applied for a job as secretary and business manager of the Broken Hill and District Hospital. When he got the job, the family were overjoyed. This was during the Depression, of course, and he hadn't been bringing in much money, and he wouldn't have to work underground anymore, so it was a great day for the family. I remember it vaguely because I was only about three at the time.

George was a great diplomat. He was careful about what he said and how he said it. He handled people with kid gloves but in a wonderful down-to-earth manner. Once when I was about ten and my sister Marie was twenty, we were both getting dressed in our shared bedroom. I was brushing my hair which was knotty and I was getting frantic because I couldn't get the knots out. In the end, I lost my temper with myself and I cracked the brush across my head. Silly idiot! Marie laughed at me. Marie was my idol; there was nobody quite like Marie, and Marie laughing at me was really the worst thing that could happen to me. So I threw the brush at her. She said, 'I'm going to tell Dad that you just lost your temper and threw your brush at me.'

'Go and tell him,' I said.

A few minutes later Dad came to me in the bedroom and said, 'I believe you lost your temper and threw your brush at Marie.'

'Yes, I did.'

'Did you hit her?'

'No, I missed.'

'Well, you'd better aim a bit better in future, hadn't you?'

That was George. You don't tell tales; you work your

problems out yourself. But all the same, when anybody had a problem, they could always go to George Gough. Everybody went to Dad with their problems about work, money or marriage. He was a wonderful counsellor and everybody loved him. I think everybody called him George, although they referred to him as Mr Gough.

I worshipped the ground he walked on. When I was a little girl, I used to sit out on the front step of the house, by the front gate, at five o'clock in the evening, waiting for him. I knew he left work at five and walked home in about fifteen minutes. I used to sit there until he turned the corner and then I ran as fast as I could down that street to meet him. I'd walk home holding his hand and when we went inside I'd help him take his coat off and I'd give it to Mum to hang up. Then I'd take his shoes off and I'd put his slippers on, then I'd give him the evening newspaper and I'd sit on his lap. That happened every night for as long as I can remember. I used to help him when he brought work home from the hospital – well, I thought I was a great help! He would be doing a lot of figure work, adding things up and writing them down, and I always sat there with the blotting paper and did all the blotting.

Every Christmas day he always went to the hospital first thing in the morning to say 'Happy Christmas' to all the people in the various wards, but my favourite thing was when he went to the children's ward. There would be a lovely Christmas Tree and Dad always distributed the Christmas presents under the tree to the children in the ward. There was always a present from the hospital to every child, apart from presents from their families. And there was always one for me as well!

Every day Dad did a complete tour of the wards, operating theatres, kitchens, X-ray rooms, every department of the hospital. He would do a complete inspection to make sure that everything was running correctly, that everything was spotlessly clean, the wards were being run well, and that everybody was getting the best possible attention.

In 1944, when I was fifteen, we went down to Robe, a lovely fishing village in South Australia, for our annual holiday at Christmas. It was really the most beautiful spot, with a population of about 300, and we had a lovely time. George completely fell in love with the place and when we got back to Broken Hill he resigned from his job at the hospital. He decided that he was going to spend the rest of his days in Robe as a fisherman. The two main fishing industries there were shark-fishing and crayfishing, and Dad became a crayfisherman. He absolutely loved it for as long as he was able to do it.

Mum wasn't at all happy about leaving Broken Hill and going down to Robe. She was a Broken Hill girl and all her friends were there, as well as Auntie Vera and Uncle Wal. But she went along with her George, and they had a lovely life down there.

Dad just loved being back at sea. He teamed up with another fellow, Charlie Fennell, and they bought a boat together. They would only fish for six months of the year but made plenty to live on. I lived down at Robe for a while but at other times I went there for holidays. Dad always looked so sun-tanned and fit. Apart from fishing, he was also very much concerned with the Robe community and its fishing industry, business-wise. As in Broken Hill, everyone in Robe adored Dad and went to him whenever they had a problem.

When I was in London in 1954 I had word from home to say that Dad had suffered a severe heart attack. He had been taken from Robe to the hospital at Kingston, twenty-seven miles away. They told me that Dad was in an oxygen tent and the doctors didn't give him much hope of recovering. All the family had gathered and it was really just a matter of time. I was most distressed that I could not be there with the family, but it was just impossible. Even had I been able to get there, I may not have made it in time. In any case, the family said, George would have wanted me to get on with my career. About a week later, I had a phone call from my sister Pat to say that Dad had made an incredible recovery. She said that the day before, they were all around his bedside and he opened his eyes and looked at them. Pat said there was a strange look on his face and she and the rest of the family are sure that he decided then and there that he was going to hold on to his life. She said that in the last twenty-four hours, he had become stronger and that the doctors were quite amazed. The family rang me regularly with details of how he was progressing. He was in hospital, in the oxygen tent, for about nine weeks, but improving slowly. The doctors were still doubtful about a full recovery and said that if he did leave the hospital he would possibly be bed-ridden and most certainly would have to use a walking-stick for the rest of his days. Well, George left hospital and did not go home to bed! He went home on a stick and, within three weeks, that was discarded. Now, that's determination for you!

Naturally, he couldn't go fishing anymore. It would have been too strenuous for him. But being an active man, he had to find some thing to keep himself occupied. So he developed two hobbies. He started teaching, free of charge, any of the children in Robe who wanted to learn to play the piano. He had quite a few pupils and they were a great interest for him. The other hobby was a most fascinating one. He constructed models of sailing ships of various types and put them into bottles of all shapes and sizes, even into small electric light bulbs. He then painted the bottles and light bulbs to give the effect of the sea and sky. They were — and still are — amazing pieces of work, or should I say, works of art. Perfect scale models. And so intricate. He did one large model which was of a schooner. She is quite splendid and is rightly housed in a glass case.

★

George and Daisy were still in Robe when I first came back to Australia in 1960 to do *The Merry Widow*, and there was great excitement. First of all, I met them in Broken Hill. They were there for a short holiday and I went out on an official visit, just to say, 'I'm back, Broken Hill, isn't it marvellous?' Our meeting at the airport was very exciting, and we had a wonderful few days together. Then they came back to Melbourne with me for the opening night of *The Merry Widow*. They had never seen me do anything of this sort before and Dad was bowled over and Mum as well, in her own way. I think it was almost too much for them to see me performing up there on the Tivoli stage and receiving such acclaim! At the party afterwards lots of people were calling Dad 'Mr Bronhill'. He absolutely loved it! He would come up to me and say, 'They're calling me "Mr Bronhill". Isn't it wonderful?' He just revelled in it.

I came back the following year to do *The Sound of Music* and once again they came over to spend some time with me in Melbourne, staying in a hotel. Once again opening night was a tremendous success and they partyed on with me and loved every minute of it. The following day, my brother John came to my hotel suite and said, 'I think Dad has just had a small stroke, just a minor one. I've been to see him and he's able to get about, but he said that when he got out of bed, he couldn't walk very well.' Immediately I asked a doctor to come over. He said that Dad had had a stroke but it was not a serious one. He must be very quiet and take things gently. I found us a nice apartment and we moved in. Dad took things very quietly, as the doctor said. He was always waiting for me when I came home every night after a performance, to find out if anyone important had been to see the show and what the reception had been like. I had to give him a run-down.

After about five weeks, one Saturday night Dad had a massive stroke and was taken to hospital. When we arrived at the hospital, St Giles, the nuns immediately recognised me and started calling Dad 'Mr Bronhill'. Even through all this, when we didn't think he would last the day, as I saw him settled into the ward and sat with him, he gave me a funny little grin and said out of the corner of his twisted mouth, 'They called me "Mr Bronhill".' He just loved that.

The doctor said to me that I should get all the family together because he didn't really think Dad would last a week. My sisters and brother all gathered and then it was just as if Dad suddenly decided, 'I'm not going to go yet,' just as he had done those years before when he had the heart attack. Like that time, he rallied. What a will power he had!

After a few weeks the hospital, of course, could not keep him there and they said he would probably have to go into a nursing home. I couldn't think of anything worse than George Gough being in a nursing home, and I knew that Mum certainly couldn't look after him. So I got in touch with the hospital in Broken Hill and spoke to Mr Nankivell, the secretary/business manager. I asked if they could possibly look after him there and Mr Nankivell said yes, of course, they would always have a bed for George Gough. So Mum, Dad, a nurse and I all flew to Broken Hill and Dad went into hospital. A flat was found for Mum because Dad's doctors said he could go home every few weeks, for a short break from the hospital atmosphere. Everything in Robe was packed up and sent to the flat in Broken Hill. Mum was in her element, in a way, because she had never wanted to leave Broken Hill in the first place. Here she was back with her old friends and the old ties again.

But it was a dreadful time for both of them. In many ways, I think Dad was sorry that he had fought so hard to live. For a man who had been so active to be suddenly bed-ridden was unbearable. He was incontinent and had to be looked after like a child. Yet he still had a good brain. Richard, my second husband, and I used to visit him at weekends. Richard would set intelligence tests of a hundred questions for him. Richard said to me, 'George really is incredible, when you think of the damage he's suffered. He still answers 80 to 85 per cent correctly.' Dad loved these little sessions with Richard. He liked Richard because he would let him do all the things nobody else would let him do, like have a cigarette.

After the first year of existing this way, George would have loved one of the doctors to help him into the next world but, of course, nobody could do that. The poor darling dwindled on for two years. All this time, dear little Daisy was struggling to help look after him. She herself was quite ill, though none of us realised just how ill, but she struggled on. At times I think she rather resented the fact that George was getting all the attention and she wasn't getting much herself. Finally, in November 1963, almost two years to the day after his stroke, the heat released George on a very hot day when the hospital air-conditioning broke down. It was a miracle, as far as I'm concerned. It was a blessing for Mum as well as for Dad because she could now get some more of the attention she deserved.

But Daisy, dear sweet soul, only lasted eight months after Dad. She died in August 1964. I was in London at the time. I was very sad that I was not able to get to her funeral.

George and Daisy were such a lovely couple. I never saw them kiss and I never heard them quarrel. We were not really a kissing family, come to think of it. When I was a kid at school, all my friends would talk about kissing their parents goodnight. I thought to myself, 'That's funny. That's something we don't do.' So that night I went to kiss Dad before I went to bed. He looked up at me and asked, 'What do you want'? I never kissed him after that; it didn't seem necessary. I did in later life, but never as a child. They were a beautiful couple, and I hope I have been the mother to my daughter that Daisy was to me, and that I can give the love, affection and guidance to my daughter that my father gave to me.

2

'Listen! The kid can sing!'

In the mining town of Broken Hill, way out in the north-west of New South Wales, Australia, at about seven in the morning of 26 June 1929, little Pat Gough was so excited. It was her eighth birthday, and her Mum and Dad had given her a special present—a baby sister called June Mary. That was me!

While you might think that an outback area in the middle of the desert might not be the most auspicious place to spend one's childhood, I can tell you that, to me, it was the most wonderful place to have been brought up. I wouldn't swap being born and bred in Broken Hill for anything in the world.

Daisy and George produced quite a few children, and what a mixed bag we all turned out to be. We were a terrifically fun-loving family. My brother John was twelve when I was born. He was a real dare-devil of a young man, with a marvellous sense of humour and, even to this day, great fun to be with.

There's a lovely story about John. Once when he was about twelve Mum sent him down to the butcher's and on his way, the coke, coal and wood man, Frosty (who, because of his job, was always a bit dirty and scruffy), had thrown a cigarette he had rolled out of his cart. There were about two-thirds of it left, so John picked it up, started smoking it and went down to the butcher's, got the meat and set off home. Suddenly, just before he got home, he thought, 'I'd better get rid of the rest of this cigarette.' Mum said, 'Have you been smoking, John?'

'No, no, Mum. I wouldn't smoke.'

'Oh, yes, you have. I can smell it on that parcel of meat.'

Eventually she got out of him that he had got the

cigarette from old Frosty. She was livid. She gave him a hiding and sent him to bed. As John said, 'Probably if the cigarette had come from somebody else it wouldn't have been quite so bad, but coming from Frosty, with his dirty hands and filthy clothes, it was really too much for Mum.'

At that time we had a lovely dog called Brownie who adored John. Brownie kept guard outside John's bedroom and refused to let Mum anywhere near him. He just sat there and growled all day. When Dad came home he said, 'What's up, Daisy? What's happened, with the dog there next to the door?' Mum explained. Dad thought he'd have to get into the room somehow, so he managed to pacify the dog and went in and gave John a good talking to. John didn't smoke any more!

My sister Marie, ten years older than me, was the rather sedate one of the family. She was quite prim and proper, lovely to look at. She ended up being my favourite sister—I suppose because she spoilt me. My sister Pat is a dear person. She has a heart of gold and will do anything for you. She was the studious one of the family. Barbara, six years older than me, was the tomboy. She had red hair, like my brother John, and she had a little bit of red-headed temper to go with it, but what terrific fun she was. Then there was me. Well, you know what I've turned out to be—a bit of a singer, a bit of an actress . . . also quite studious.

Before I was born, however, there were two other children. The first one was Marjorie, who was born before John, and who died from a convulsion when she was about eight months old. My other sister, Valerie, if she had lived would have been the closest to me in age. She would have been about four years older than me.

One day a little funeral went by as my mother was talking to a nextdoor neighbour. They could see that it was a tiny coffin. My mother said, 'Oh, the poor mother and family of that dear little child! I couldn't bear it if anything happened to my Valerie!' Two weeks later, they were burying Valerie. She had contracted diptheria and didn't last very long.

My earliest vivid recollection is of my third birthday. I was having a little afternoon party and somebody had given me a lovely baby doll. I was absolutely out of my mind for this doll. I wouldn't let it alone all afternoon. I didn't eat any jellies, I didn't eat any cakes, I didn't eat anything! I just sat down on my own, nursing my little doll and gazing lovingly into its eyes. I think that was probably an early indication of what I'm like now. I absolutely adore children and I should have been surrounded by them.

Our nextdoor neighbours, Mr and Mrs Herbert, and dear Grandma Beaumont and Uncle Norm Beaumont, were the first to hear of my birth. Pat ran straight in and told them about her baby sister. They became very much a part of my life. As I grew up I used to run in and tell Aunty Herdie and Uncle Bob (as I used to call them) everything that was going on in my life. I suppose that day, my third birthday, I would have dashed straight in to Aunty Herdie and showed the doll to her. Mind you, she was probably at the party. That family became like a second family to me.

Grandma was the most fantastic cook imaginable. She used to make the most marvellous scones and cakes, and they were quite delicious. Often there would just be a little call over the fence: 'June Jerry!' – that's what they used to call me, sometimes just 'Jerry' – 'Come and see what Grandma's made.' I'd be over the fence like a bolt of lightning.

Uncle Norm used to play the piano and he also had an extraordinary instrument like a rod with little legs. When you held it, you could play up and down on the keys of the piano and it played all the chords, so you never had to think about playing in the right key. It automatically did it and you could just sing and accompany yourself with this little thing. I just adored that thing and before I ever had any piano lessons, I used to go in there regularly and play the piano. Mum and Dad had to work hard to get me home!

About this time Dad bought our first piano. I suppose I was only about three or four then. Dad played the piano very well and had a lovely natural singing voice, so that was

14

the beginning of what we called our sing-songs around the piano every weekend.

One night when I was about four, Mum was putting me to bed while Dad was in the living-room playing the piano. He was playing a song that I obviously must have heard him sing many times before because suddenly I sang it all the way through, absolutely word-perfect. Mum was bowled over. She called out, 'George, listen! The kid can sing!' Dad said, 'Daisy, bring her out here.' So I was propped up by the piano in my pyjamas and I sang the song straight through again. It was called 'The Dear Little Shamrock', and that was the start of my singing career. Now I'm fifty-eight, so that means I've been singing pretty well non-stop for fifty-four years!

When I was five I started school at Central School which was only about three blocks away. My kindergarten days are vivid in my memory. Even then it was quite obvious that I loved singing because nobody could stop me! I was always singing a little tune. The other things I loved at kindergarten were painting and drawing. Our teacher was Miss Bax. I really loved her and she thought I wasn't too bad either! So my school days got off to a really lovely beginning.

When I was about five, going to school for the first time, one of the boys in the class used to follow me home every afternoon. His name was Johnny Hardy. He kept trying to make conversation with me, trying to hold my hand, and I couldn't bear him anywhere near me. I've no idea why, because he was really a lovely boy and very clever. All the girls used to say I was very lucky that Johnny Hardy wanted to follow me home. But I kept brushing him off and he persisted. So I used to try to get away from school quickly and take devious routes home, which was ridiculous because we only lived a few blocks away, but he'd find me somewhere. Eventually I had to tell him that I didn't care about him so he gave up trying to woo me.

About a year later I felt dreadful because Johnny got meningitis and was desperately ill. I didn't ever see him after

15

that and I always felt guilty that I hadn't been kinder to him. I do hope he has forgiven me after all these years.

My mother was a Catholic and my father was Church of England, but Mum wanted us to be baptised Catholics, so we were and we were brought up as Catholics. Apart from me, all the children went to the Catholic school. There is a lovely story about Barbara which came back to Dad through one of the nuns. When Barb was in kindergarten, at the end of the day one of the children was asked to stay behind and sweep the classroom. After a couple of weeks it was Barb's turn. The nun said, 'It's your turn to sweep the classroom. You stay behind tonight.' Barbara just sat there. When the nun asked her to sweep the classroom she refused.

'Barbara, when Jesus was a little boy, if he'd been asked to sweep the classroom, he would have done it,' said the nun.

'Yes, but I'm not Jesus,' replied Barbara.

Every Wednesday morning at nine o'clock we had to attend scripture class. Naturally each religion went to its own particular class — me to the Catholic class. Once, somewhere about the beginning of the war — when I was about ten or eleven — the woman who taught scripture started saying that the Germans and Italians were Catholic races and so our sympathies should lie with them. We must pray to God that the Germans and Italians won the war. Well, I found this quite the most extraordinary thing that I had ever heard, so, when Dad came home from work that night, I immediately told him what had been said. He got in touch with the headmistress and explained why I wouldn't be attending scripture classes any more.

Mum's sister, Aunty Vera, and her husband, Uncle Wal, and their three children, Moira, Geraldine and Noel, lived in Broken Hill and we used to spend lots of lovely weekends with them. Moira, or Moisie, as I used to call her, was about my age and we always spent every Sunday together. One Sunday I'd go over to her place and the other Sundays she'd come over to my place. It seemed like an enormous trek across Broken Hill. But we would walk across, pushing our

16

little dolls' prams with our dolls in them, and then stop off at the lolly shop. We always had sixpence to spend, so with my money I would always buy sixpence worth of lollies and when I got to Moisie's we'd share them out. We'd do the same thing in reverse the following week. We played Mothers and Fathers, and Nurses and Doctors, and you name it, we played it.

The two families visited each other regularly. We used to play poker and even when I was nine and ten or in my early teens I was allowed to play penny poker. I was allowed to save up a few pennies every week. We used to have marvellous games. Dad was a clever bluffer so he invariably won. He kept his winnings in an old black sock!

I sang at my first concert – just a little gathering – when I was about five. I sang a lovely little Scottish air, 'Comin' Through the Rye'. But my real stage debut was when I was six. This was in the big Crystal Theatre in Broken Hill, and I sang a song called 'Little Man, You've Had a Busy Day'. I was done up in white tie and tails and a top hat, and I had a cane underneath my arm. Cheeky as they come, I picked out a lovely man in the front row and played the whole song to him. The cheek of the devil, even at six!

When I was about eight or nine, I invented my favourite game, which I played on my own. I discovered that by rolling up a piece of tin into the shape of a megaphone, I could talk and sing into it and get a lovely resonant, echoing sound, as if it were a radio. So I started playing radio stations, in which I played all the characters. I was the radio announcer, and I did quite good impressions of people like Gracie Fields, Deanna Durbin, Judy Garland and an American boy singer called Bobby Breen who used to sing a song called 'The Rainbow on the River'. I think, already in my mind, the idea had formed that one day I would be on the stage or singing on the radio, perhaps just in Broken Hill.

Over the years my repertoire developed. I sang first of all 'The Dear Little Shamrock', then I went on to 'Comin Through the Rye', 'Robin Adair' and 'Cockles and Mussels'.

17

Around this time my sister Marie used to sing as well. Marie had quite a lovely voice but unfortunately her repertoire never got beyond 'The Mountains of Mourne'. Marie absolutely hated 'The Mountains of Mourne' after a few years and she couldn't bear it when she was asked to sing it. Later a similar thing happened to me. When I was eleven somebody arrived at our house with a copy of a song called 'Vilja' from *The Merry Widow*. They thought it would be a nice song for me to learn and gave it to my father to teach me. So I learnt 'Vilja' and *everywhere* I went after that, whether it was just at a local concert or at somebody's house or a party, I was always asked to sing 'Vilja'. I kept singing that song pretty well non-stop until I was seventeen and a half, by which time I loathed it. I vowed and declared that I'd never sing that song again as long as I lived!

Around that time we used to have a club called the Smilers' Club. It was held at Johnson's Picture Theatre every Wednesday from four o'clock to five o'clock and was broadcast by 2BH. We had to apply, audition and ask whether we would be accepted to perform on the show. It was great! I sang many times, lovely songs like 'Somewhere Over the Rainbow' from *The Wizard of Oz* and 'One Day When We were Young', 'Because' and 'I'll Walk Beside You', which I sang at lots of weddings when I was about fourteen or fifteen. They were great days and I think they stood me in good stead for my future career.

During my primary school days it was obvious that I was pretty clever. I learned quickly and I really did enjoy my school days. There was no 'Oh, do I have to go to school?' or making out I was sick. I was happy to go there and happy to do homework. I suppose it was partly because my darling father was such a great help to me. He would teach me ways of studying, easy learning methods. He had an excellent mind and was a clever man himself. He loved helping all of us, particularly with our school work.

At the end of primary school, I was dux. So when I was twelve and a half I went to Broken Hill High School. I don't know why, but instead of doing languages, I chose to do the commercial course. Apart from the usual studies of maths, English, history, geography and science, I was learning things like book-keeping, sewing, cooking and shorthand and typing. I was absolutely hopeless at these last two subjects. While the other girls were doing so many words per minute, I was doing so many minutes per word. But I was clever at maths. I even used to get sick of myself because I could always solve the problems by the time the teacher had finished writing up the problem on the board. I was also very good at English, geography and history, but not terribly good in science. I was not too bad in chemistry but was hopeless in physics.

When I was about fourteen a new teacher for geography and history, a man called Mr Koffel, arrived at school. He sometimes doubled up with maths and English as well. He was wonderful, a great character, not frantically good-looking but such a marvellous person. I really rather fell for Sam Koffel.

I always went home at lunch-time for a lunch of delicious hot bread straight from the baker with butter melting all over it and home-made jam. One lunch-time my sister Barbara was home and I said, 'We've got the most marvellous new teacher. He is absolutely dishie, really divine. He's called Mr Koffel.'

'I believe he's going to a party I'm going to tonight,' said Barbara.

'Eyes off! I saw him first.'

The following morning, over breakfast Barbara said, 'June, you know your Mr Koffel? He brought me home from the party last night, and he is rather lovely, isn't he? He's great fun.'

'Yes, but I'm not pleased with this, Barbara.'

'Oh, it probably won't come to anything, I'll leave him to you, but I am seeing him again.'

Well, of course, they got married, didn't they?

I didn't have many boyfriends, really, during my school

days, but a couple stand out vividly in my mind. One of them, who is now a solicitor in Broken Hill, was one of the sons of the town clerk. His name was John Crowley. I got to know the family very well and quite often at the weekends I'd end up at the Crowleys' house and we'd all cook together. John used to pester me a bit. He would ride up and down outside our place on his bicycle, and he used to drive me round the bend slightly. I loved going to the Crowleys' occasionally but didn't want to be really caught up. I saw John recently. We had a marvellous time laughing at stories of when we were young and he fancied me.

During this time I really was very clever and I had a quick mind. I used to work a lot with my father on homework and, as I've said, he would teach me ways to learn things quickly. All of these things have stood me in very good stead for learning my roles. Even today I can learn something quite quickly. In those days at school one sat for IQ tests every year, and I found out many years later from Sam Koffel that when I was fifteen and sixteen, I had the highest IQ in New South Wales!

In my second year at high school we had a marvellous new music teacher called Miss Marjorie Earnshaw. She was absolutely splendid, a marvellous musician. She assembled the all-girl Broken Hill High School choir which really was tremendous. (The boys wouldn't have anything to do with things like that. It was a bit sissy!) Because I had a very strong voice for such a young person, I was asked to sing third part – the lowest part – so in all the numbers that we learnt I generally sang the deeper line, except that in solos I would sing the higher line, the soprano solo. Eventually, in my second and third years, we entered the City of Sydney Eisteddfod in the School Choir section and walked off with every prize.

Miss Earnshaw was a wonderful woman and she got the best out of us. We all loved her very much. The other thing that she decided to do – apart from school concerts (at which I sang 'Vilja', of course!) – was our first musical comdey, in

1943. We had done scenes from plays, and scenes from Gilbert and Sullivan, but we'd never done a full musical comedy before. It was decided to do Lionel Monkton's *A Country Girl*. The boys wouldn't participate in *anything*, so we girls had to play all the male roles and, would you believe, I played the leading man, Commander Geoffrey Challoner of the Royal Navy. Somebody the other day sent me a copy of the notice in our school magazine, *Quondong*, for *The Country Girl*. It said: 'Handling a male role, that of Commander Challoner, June Gough acted and sang with a remarkable poise and naturalness and her duet with Betty McDonald as Marjorie being excellently toned.' How about that!

The family had intended that I finish school in third year, after I'd got my intermediate certificate, but I had such a good pass in the intermediate that they decided that it would be a good idea if I carried on my schooling until I matriculated at the end of fifth year. Subjects that I'd been doing for the commercial course, shorthand and typing, and home course subjects like cooking and sewing, were not carried through to fourth and fifth years so I had to choose two other subjects. I had two choices: I could choose between technical drawing and Latin, and I didn't fancy doing five years Latin in two years, so I chose technical drawing. The other choice was between theory of music and French, and naturally because I was interested in music and singing I chose theory of music, for which I'm very sorry these days. French would have been handy to me as far as singing was concerned, whereas while I know an augmented fifth from a diminished fourth, I don't think it's of any use to me whatsoever.

The funny thing about the technical drawing class was that it was extraordinary in those days for a girl to take a boys' subject. I was the first girl ever in Australia to take that course. When we started in fourth year there were seventeen boys in the class and me, and by the time we got to matriculation in fifth year there were two boys left and me. Would you believe that out of the two boys and me, I think I was the only one to pass in technical drawing! It was amazing how I could put together nuts and bolts and do cross-sections of them, probably because I loved drawing. Then I did five years of theory of music in two years. So those two years of schooling were exhausting but I pulled through. I think I failed chemistry but I passed in every other subject. But an academic career was definitely not for me. I knew that the only thing I wanted to do was sing.

After Mum and Dad left Broken Hill I lived with my sister Barbara who by now had married Sam Koffel. When I was in fourth year they left because Sam was offered a post in Orange and I went to live with my sister Marie who was also married by then. I always went down to Robe for my holidays and had a wonderful time.

In Robe I was always asked to sing at dances and parties. A local chap there who was a bit older than me, Ron Went, had a marvellous natural singing voice, a tenor. We became a duo. We always danced together and sang along with the music. Everyone asked for more. We never really had a great romantic affair but we loved each other's company and loved singing together. Ron Went could have made a career with his voice because it was a wonderful natural sound. His wife, Helen, still says she always felt she was very lucky to get him away from me.

When I finished school I went to live in Robe with Mum and Dad for nearly a year. I got a job as receptionist in the Robe Hotel. It was an ordinary old place but it was wonderful fun being there. We had an incredible man called Noel Domaschenz as the chef. He always over-catered, particularly in the sweets line, so every day when I was sitting in my office, Noel would arrive and say, 'June, what are we going to call yesterday's strawberry fool?' We'd have to think up new names for all the sweets so that people didn't realise until they'd received their serving that it was exactly the same as they had yesterday!

When I was about seventeen a young man I adored came

into my life – Brian Sowry. Actually I had been attracted to him first when I was much younger, about nine or ten. Before his voice broke he had the most beautiful pure boy soprano you could imagine. I liked going to a particular mass every Sunday because Brian used to sing in the choir and I loved hearing him sing all the solos in the cathedral in Broken Hill.

Brian's family were charming, too. We all called his father Doc and his mother, Kathy, was always lovely to me. We were good friends. Brian would come up to our place nearly every Sunday morning and we'd sit and read the Sunday papers and laugh over the comics. I used to call him Sad Sack because one of the comic strips was called 'Sad Sack' and Brian always looked a bit like a sad sack, even though he had the most twinkling eyes. He had a happy downward smile on his face. He remained Sad Sack to me for a long time. In his room Brian had a record-player and we used to play records and dance and sing. He also played the piano very well. His voice had a marvellous rather deep sound and we used to have lovely sing-songs. He was part of a group that used to get together at weekends and have jam-sessions. Brian would play the piano, we had a man called Bamber on guitar, Bobby Chalmers on saxophone, somebody on drums and I used to sing. Josie Bock would be forever getting us lemonades. It was at Bockie's house that we used to gather. Her parents, whom we called Maw and Paw, were absolute gems the way they put up with our racket.

Sometime later, when Brian and I were a little older, we maintained a warm relationship. Once, when I was about nineteen, Brian had just bought himself a lovely sportscar, a very swish white MG. We decided to visit my parents in Robe. On the last lap, about a hundred miles from Robe, it started to rain. The windscreen wipers started to play up and we went quite a distance with them hardly working at all. How we ever got there I'll never know. Brian used to go at quite a speed and when we arrived in Robe, we charged down the main street and skidded to a stop outside Mum and Dad's house. Within about fifteen minutes the local policeman had arrived to say, 'Will you be careful not to go round the streets at anything more than thirty miles per hour?' Brian was smartly put in his place!

When it became obvious that my singing career was going to take first place in my life, my romance with Brian finished. The funny thing is that when I married, I married a Brian and when Brian married, he married a June. There must be something Freudian there!

When I was about eighteen or nineteen and was working at one of the department stores in Broken Hill, my brother John and I were living with my sister Marie. I went to a dance one night and got home fairly late—I suppose about 12.30—and when I woke up in the morning both Marie and John asked why I'd been out so late. I said, 'We'd been to the dance and we were having a bit of fun.' They asked how I got home. I said, 'Somebody drove me home.' They asked who and I said, 'Les Liveley.'

'What? You let Les Liveley drive you home? Don't you know about his reputation?'

'No. I think he's very nice. We had a lot of fun and talked and laughed a bit. He drove me home and kissed me goodnight.'

'He is the biggest flirt in Broken Hill! How could you?'

They were absolutely furious with me and I didn't feel I'd done anything wrong. To me, Les was very sophisticated compared with some of the others I'd known. I was terribly upset and they were really scolding me as if I was a little girl instead of nineteen. I said to Marie, 'I don't want to go to work today. I don't feel at all well.' She said, 'You *are* going to work. You're just putting this on. You can stay there for an hour and we'll see how you are. I'll phone the store and say you'll be late in.' Within an hour I was covered in spots! I had chicken pox and they couldn't do enough for me then.

I didn't see Les very often. His family had a delicatessen in Argent Street (the main street of Broken Hill) and I used

George and Daisy Gough on their wedding day. *Left to right:* Grandfather Hall (Daisy's father), George Gough (*seated*), Uncle Cecil, Daisy Gough, Daisy's sisters, Lil and Vera (she hated that hat!).

George Gough, father.

One of the model ships father proudly made.

June Gough, aged eight, a picture taken by her brother John.

June and her cousin Monica with their pet kangaroo, Rougie.

June aged twelve, in a favourite outfit.

June, aged 14, as Commander Geoffrey
Challoner of the Royal Navy in *A Country
Girl* in Broken Hill.

to drop in to see Les and his brother Max occasionally. One Saturday afternoon Les said, 'I want to take you out to the golf course.'

'What for? I can't play golf.'

'We're not playing golf, and besides nobody ever goes there.'

And when I got there and saw the golf course I was not surprised – just dirt everywhere and a few tacky saltbushes. I said, 'Why have you brought me out here, Les?'

'There's a funny noise in the car and I want you to drive. Have you ever driven a car?'

'No, I've never even sat behind a steering wheel!'

'It's quite easy. I'll get it going, then you sit in the seat and steer because I want to lean out and look underneath and see where this clanging noise is coming from. Just keep the car going very slowly and keep on this path.

'There's one problem though, June – the steering column is sort of back to front, so if you have to turn right, you have to turn the wheel to the left and vice versa.'

I got behind the wheel and we started. Well, of course, my natural instinct, if I wanted to turn right, was to turn the wheel right! I was petrified and screamed at him. I said, 'I'm sorry, I can't do this anymore. How do I stop this thing?'

He *did* find out what the clanging noise was, which was something. But it took a long while for me to be brave enough to get behind a steering wheel again, thanks to Les.

3

'You have a fine gift—see that you don't fail the giver'

When I was about fifteen I heard that there was a good singing teacher in Broken Hill called Mrs Molly Carrack-Morgan, so I asked her if she would give me some lessons and she seemed happy to do so. She said that she wouldn't teach me anything about actual singing because she was of the belief that the voice had to find its own way at so young an age, but she would help me with a lot of other aspects of singing and performing. I agree entirely with her. I think it's the most important thing for young singers not to let anybody interfere with their voice until they are about eighteen or nineteen because the voice has to settle and, as she said, find its own way. So I started working with her and she was really strict, unbelievably strict. Her house was situated next to the convent and she used to get very cross because the tennis courts were on the side of her house where she gave her lessons and kids were always knocking tennis balls into her windows. She never threw them back—she kept them. She was really quite a vicious old thing at times.

She taught me an extraordinary amount about diction. She said, 'You must never think that you are just singing to the people in the front row. You must think of the people right in the last row of any theatre or hall where you may ever sing.' I think she must have had some inkling even then that things would happen for me by way of a professional singing career. She said, 'Project. Think of the ends of words. Cross your t's, dot your i's almost, so that everybody can hear and understand exactly what you're singing *about*.' The other thing that she taught me a great deal about was phrasing of songs – how to turn a phrase beautifully to great effect – and she taught me a great deal about the importance of words. She said to me that if you think of the words that you're singing about and really feel the importance of the words, quite often the sound will look after itself. That, I think, is one of the best things that I have ever been taught. And I say this to many young singers today who talk to me about singing. I say the most important thing is *what you are singing about*. So many singers are so concerned with the sound that they are making that they are not interested in the full importance of what they are singing about.

Over the years so many people have commented on the things that this wonderful woman in Broken Hill taught me. They comment on my diction, my phrasing, my sense of style and on the way I use the words so importantly and the way that I feel for words.

Mrs Carrack-Morgan was in charge of one of the two big choirs in Broken Hill, called the Philharmonic Society, which was a male and female choir. The other one was an all-male choir called the Quartet Club. Now both of these singing clubs gave about three concerts each a year to which they invited what we called the 'stars' from the 'big cities' – important people who were working on radio and doing big concerts around Australia and appearing in a professional capacity. But they also invited a local artist to sing as a guest, and when I was sixteen I sang at my first big concert which was for Mrs Molly Carrack-Morgan's Philharmonic Society. I received the princely sum of two guineas and I thought that was absolutely marvellous – I thought I was made. At the ripe old age of sixteen I sang an aria from *The Barber of Seville* – 'Una Voce Poco Fa' – and I sang a couple of ballads – 'Birdsongs at Eventide' and I think 'Comin' Through the Rye' – and everybody thought that I was the cat's whiskers. I was bowled over by the reception and I thought, 'There might be something to this after all – it might all happen.' As a result of that, the Quartet Club asked me to sing for them as well. Once again, my performances were highly acclaimed and I thought it was too good to be true. Consequently, about three years later when I had finished my schooling, I decided that it was all very well being the golden-haired girl of the Silver City (as Broken Hill is known) but that I should really go off to Sydney and see what happened to me in the 'big smoke'.

So I arrived in Sydney in January 1949. I was nineteen; I turned twenty in June 1949. I had been told of a singing teacher in Sydney called Hector Fleming so I went along and sang for him. He appeared to be impressed with me. He said he would teach me and gave me a scholarship. So I started having lessons with Mr Fleming and all went well for quite a while. We worked strongly on a couple of arias, in particular, because I had heard about the City of Sydney Eisteddfod and the Sydney Sun Aria competition, which was open to professionals and amateurs. Eventually my heat for the Sun Aria came up and I sang 'Una Voce Poco Fa' from *The Barber of Seville*—the same one that I had sung at the concert in Broken Hill.

At the end of the heats, which were held in the Conservatorium of Music, one of the members of the Eisteddfod committee came on to announce the semi-finalists. They had announced the various numbers—we were not names, just numbers, and I was No. 179—and then I was rather shattered to hear them say that competitor No. 179 would have been included in the semi-finals except that she had not sung her aria in the original key. I didn't realise that you had to sing them in the original key and 'Una Voce Poco Fa' was originally written in the key of E flat. In *The Barber of Seville* the leading role is written in a coloratura mezzo soprano but it is often performed by a coloratura soprano, so I had sung it in the coloratura soprano key which was a key higher—in the key of F. So, not to be outdone, with all the cheek imaginable, I quickly sent a message around to the adjudicators to ask if they would let me sing it again if I could find a copy of it in the original key. So the word came back—yes, they would let me sing it again. The person who had made the announcement about the semi-finalists then told the audience what had happened and a great cheer went up. Out I went and sang it in the original key. And I got into the semi-finals. I don't know who I ousted—maybe they had an extra semi-finalist that year!

The night of the finals eventually came around. They always announce the places from last up to first. And it came to three of us being left there—myself, a baritone called Harold Whitlock and Joan Sutherland. Well, I was third, Whitlock was second and Sutherland first—but, would you believe, there was only one point between first and third, so I nearly won it my first time up! I always say I was in great company, though, with Joan.

Mr Fleming was highly delighted with all of this and we returned to ordinary lessons. One of the things that he started to do was teaching me to sing things that I knew were too heavy for my voice. For instance, at the ripe old age of twenty, as I was then, he was teaching me to sing things like 'Ritorna Vincitor' from *Aida* and I knew that this was completely wrong for me—it was much too dramatic and heavy for my voice. And the other thing that started to happen was that he became a little free with his hands. I didn't like this but didn't know how to handle it. I was not paying for my lessons but I thought I had to get away from all this because I was an innocent girl from Broken Hill and I didn't like men touching me up! So I thought I'd have to break away because otherwise I'd become neurotic and that's something that I've never been and never will be. I had heard of a singing teacher called Madame Marianne Mathy and somebody I'd met who studied with her said, 'I'm sure she'd love to hear you—as a matter of fact, she's been after you ever since you came third in the Aria competition.' Mathy was highly delighted that I wanted to study with her. Then, of course, I had to tell Mr Fleming that I was leaving. I thanked him very much for his generosity in teaching me for nothing but I said I felt that the type of arias he wanted me to study now were completely wrong for me and I had to find somebody who would teach me in the manner that I thought I should be taught.

So I joined the Mathy school. She was unbelievable — half French, half German — a martinet. I got on very well with her, I suppose partly because we were both Cancerians, and she felt a great love for me almost immediately. And I thought she was pretty fantastic because I was, as you've no doubt gathered, a pretty cheeky kid, and I knew how to handle things so that if she ever got very stroppy with me, I would just laugh it off. I'd been told by lots of other students of hers that at some stage of the game she'd have you in floods of tears because 'she's so evil and wicked and nasty to you'. So I was prepared.

Madame Mathy and I started working hard on vocalisations and she started teaching me some arias which were much more suitable for my voice. Naturally I entered for the Sydney Sun Aria again that year, 1950, and we worked very hard on a wonderful aria from *Manon*, an opera by the French composer Massenet. That year I also did the 'Una Voce' from *The Barber of Seville* once again. So we worked and worked. She really was the slave-driver of all time. I was then working at the NRMA in the city centre but living in Bankstown with my sister Barbara and her husband Sam Koffel. I would work all day at the NRMA, then I would go out in the evening for a lesson with Marianne, then I'd get a bus from her place to Central Station and a train out to Bankstown. We were getting very close to the semi-finals. One night she really was driving me like there was no tomorrow — absolutely screaming at me and pulling me apart — and I got to the stage that so many people had told me about — with the tears. They were almost there — the lump in the throat — and I was getting so upset, with myself and with her because she was being so nasty to me. I pulled myself together. I looked at her and said,'You're not going to make me cry, you bloody bitch.' She said, 'Oh darling, this is wonderful. You have got ze temperament to become a good singer, to have a profession as a singer. I love you very dearly, you are good girl. Now go home – we won't work anymore.' So I went home. I made it into the finals.

Then, a couple of weeks later, before the finals, we'd had a gruelling working session and I was very nervy and edgy because it was a great thing for me to be in the finals the second year. I hoped desperately, of course, that I would win it. And she said, 'Darling, I give you some tablets, I give you a tablet to take now on your way home and you relax and you'll be wonderful. And here's another one for you to have tonight when you go to bed.' So I took this tablet at her place – it was a Valium – I didn't know the first thing about these things. Well, I made it to Central Station and caught the train and it appears that I must have fallen asleep because I woke up at the train depot. I'd gone straight through Bankstown where I should have got off and I had to find my way back. I didn't take the second tablet, I can assure you – that was enough for me.

Well, the night of the Sun Aria finals arrived and it was a great night. They went through the various lower placings and we got to the last three – Patricia Baird, Majorie Conley and myself, all coloratura sopranos. Patricia Baird came third and I said, 'It's you, Marjorie,' because I thought she was marvellous. She had sung the 'Marten aller Arten' from *Il Seraglio* by Mozart as her main aria and it was quite stunning. But I was absolutely bowled over when it was Marjorie who came second and I came first. The difference between first and third on that occasion was twelve points so I thought I'd even done a little better than Joan Sutherland.

My adjudication from Sir Bernard Heinze for the aria 'Gavotte' from *Manon* said:

> Here for the first time tonight is the characteristic vocal quality of the language of the aria. This has been constantly absent with the previous singers. There is an immediate grasp, too, of the nature and meaning of the role in the singer's interpretation. Personal as well as vocal characterisation are one of the attributes of this young singer – fine style and artistic intuitiveness are evident.

And for the 'Una Voce' from *The Barber of Seville* he said:

> The same remarks apply here with a noticeable change in the colour
> of the voice in the use of Italian. Musically and temperamentally,
> this young singer is fitted to sing with orchestra. Pitch is good;
> tempo within the expressive moves of rubato is rational and
> reasonably controlled. The characterisation of the role of Rosina
> is sung with splendid verve and understanding. This is a voice
> of quite exceptional distinction and promise. It is worthy of every
> encouragement. I feel inclined to parody Schumann and say 'Hats
> off, gentlemen – a singer'. You have a fine gift – see that you don't
> fail the giver.

And I was twenty-one at the time – the youngest person ever
to have won the Sydney Sun Aria competition – and,
incidentially, I still am!

After I won the Sydney Sun Aria Mathy did two
important things with me. The first was that she helped me
change my name. The 'ough' pronunciation of Gough can
be 'oh', 'ow', 'oo', 'uff' or whatever you want, so I got June
Gow, June Go, or June Goo in Sydney, but very rarely did
I get June 'Goff'. One day I went to Mathy and I said,
'Madame, I think I would like to change my name.'

She said, 'Oh, darling, I am so pleased. I have never liked
this name Gough.'

'Well, I'm sorry, but that's what I was born.'

'Well, I'm happy. Now what do you think you are going
to do?'

'I thought that since Broken Hill has raised all this lovely
money to help me go overseas, I would like to change my
name to have something to do with Broken Hill.'

'Oh, wonderful idea, my darling. Now tell me about this
place, Broken Hill.'

'Well, as you know, it's a mining town. One of the things
about it is that all the streets are named after minerals and
ores.'

'Tell me the name of some of these streets.'

'There's Sulphide Street, Bromide Street, Oxide Street,
Iodide Street, Galena Street . . .'

'Darling, these are terrible names. What was the name of the street where you were born?'

'Wolfram Street.'

'June Wolfram—no, I don't think so.'

'I don't either.'

'But, darling, with all these names, there must be something pretty, something nice.'

'Well, the only really pretty name is Crystal Street.'

She thought for a minute or two. 'Oh, darling, I have got it—we will call you Belle Crystal.'

Well, I mean to say, it sounds like something out of a Wild West saloon bar. I said, 'No way, darling,' and she said, 'Well, what about Crystal Belle?' and I said, 'No, darling, definitely not.'

So a week went past. Then, quite early one morning, the phone went at my sister's place (where I was staying). It was Marianne, wanting to talk to me. 'Darling, I have got it,' she said.

'What have you got, Madame? What's the matter?'

'No, no, no, no. I have got your new name.'

'Oh, what is it?'

'June Bronhill—we cut out the "K" and the "E" from Broken and we run them all together and we have Bronhill.'

So it was her, that wonderful woman, who came up with my name.

The other thing that Mathy did was that she decided my eyebrows were too thick! One night I was doing a performance in the Sydney Town Hall with the Sydney Symphony Orchestra which Joseph Post conducted, and Mathy had decided that that was the time she was going to attack my eyebrows. So she sat me down, got a pair of tweezers and plucked away for all she was worth. I was left with two slim arched eyebrows. I was a bit shattered myself, because it just didn't look like me suddenly. And that night my sister Barbara was attending. She came into the dressing-room before the concert and she was absolutely bowled over.

'God, June, what's happened to your eyebrows?' she said.

33

'Madame has just plucked them.'

'Oh, dreadful!' she said.

Then Marianne came into the dressing-room. Barbara turned on her and said, 'What have you done to our girl?' But I'm so glad that Marianne did that because my eyebrows really were quite bushy, as you can possibly see from the odd photograph! Now, of course, there's hardly anything there at all—I just draw them in—but it makes a lot of difference to my eyes.

Mathy was really quite the most amazing woman—we worked like crazy together. We became very close and she actually called herself my foster mother. She had the most unbelievable energy and personality, and I have some lovely stories about her. She had a marvellous friend, Walter Jacobsen, who had come out from Germany much about the same time as she did, following hotfot on Mathy and her husband. Walter was a darling and he had been her lover, living in the same house as Marianne and her husband for fifteen years—talk about a *ménage à trois*! Walter was divine. He had the most delightful sense of humour and everybody loved him. I think I only saw the husband once or twice. Mathy was a volatile and sexy woman, and lots of the young men who came for lessons were in fear and trepidation on many occasions because she would back them up against the wall and get them to kiss her. They didn't want to, but they felt they had to!

One of Marianne's students was a young man called Neville Grave. Neville has a lovely tone of voice and he's a dear friend of mine now. Some years later, when I had already gone to England, Neville's father died. He was very upset because his family were very close. After a while, Neville went back to lessons and was quite upset that Mathy kept picking on him about this, that and the other. He was just taking it and feeling quite miserable generally until she really said the worst thing imaginable. You see, Marianne always liked men, but not so much women, and she turned to Neville and said, 'It was a pity that it was your father that

34

died and not your mother.' Now, Neville adored his mother. He just picked up his music, tears streaming down his cheeks, and he turned to her and said, 'You are a fucking old bitch!' and walked out. He was walking up the road towards his car and Marianne came running out of the house and up the street, calling, 'Neville, Neville, Neville darling, don't go, don't go, Neville darling, come back here, Neville, don't go, don't go.' He thought, 'I'd better stop, otherwise she'll bring all the neighbours out.' So he stopped, and she went up to him and said, 'Darling, fucking I love; bitch I know I am; but old, how can you be so cruel?' That was Mathy to a 'T'.

This extraordinary woman also expected everybody to be at her beck and call. For instance, if she was just going up the road to Double Bay (where she lived) to have her hair done, she would telephone Neville, who lived perhaps twenty minutes away from her by car, and say, 'Neville, come over here. I have to go the hairdresser's, I want you to drive me to the hairdresser's.' You never said no. Neville would get in the car and drive over and take her to the hairdresser's. She would say, 'I will be about an hour, Neville. Wait for me and then take me home.' I would suddenly get a phone call: 'Darling, I feel like going out for dinner. You come and collect me and we go to Double Bay and we have dinner.' Even if you had something planned, you never said, 'Well, Madame, I'm sorry I can't possibly do that,' because you just had to go there.

Even though she was a darling, she had very little sense of humour, whereas Walter had the most delightful sense of humour. One Christmas Day they were with my dear friend Rex (Freddie) and myself and one of the repetiteur conductors from the Australian Opera Company, Russell Channel. We were sitting round having a lovely luncheon and talking about the Australian Opera Company, when Russell suddenly said, 'You know, the chorus get more money than I do.' Walter said, 'Well, there are a lot more of them.' We all fell about laughing but Marianne said, 'What

35

is so funny? What you laughing about? Wally, Wally—what you say that's so funny?' When we'd said it again for her, she still didn't understand what it was all about.

After 1952 my base was in London, but whenever I came back to Australia for any shows or any work of any kind I always made sure that I worked with Marianne because she was such a fantastic singing teacher. What she didn't know about voice production was really not worth thinking about. And it was on one such occasion, when I was home, that she phoned me one morning and said that Walter had died suddenly and she was deeply upset. Over the next six months I saw an incredible decline in her. She had lost one of the dearest things in her life, a beautiful person who had loved her, who had tolerated her temperaments and still had remained. Some months later, I was in Sydney preparing for a show and I went to see her. She said to me, 'Darling, I have no wish to live any longer. I can hardly play the piano, my hands are riddled with arthritis, the retina in both my eyes have gone, I cannot see well, I have no purpose in life anymore.'

I said, 'Yes, you have, darling, you still know so much about singing.'

'Yes, but I cannot play the piano.'

'But you can afford to employ somebody to play the piano.'

'No, darling, I cannot, I cannot, it is too expensive and I am cranky. I cannot give to the people what I want to give because I am not happy.'

I said, 'Whenever I'm in Sydney I will come to your lessons and I will help you because you have quite often asked me to come and work with you with certain students.' These were students who she thought had tremendous potential but she felt she was not getting through to them because she was getting old—she was eighty-seven or eighty-eight— but she had more energy and more knowledge of singing than a lot of people a third of her age.

And I tried and I tried. I said, 'Come on, darling, you

must work,' and she said, 'No, I'm going to finish it.' So I went to see her every day of that week, trying to say, 'No, darling, you mustn't do anything silly.'

I was opening a show on the Saturday night and I had tickets for her. She said to me, 'I will not be there, darling. I will give the tickets to a young girl who is helping to look after me and she will take her boyfriend. I want you to take them out to dinner and keep them away from the house until early morning.'

I said, 'No, Marianne, you mustn't do these silly things, you mustn't.'

'You come to see me on Saturday morning before you go to your theatre.'

I called in and I said goodbye to her. I didn't know what to do myself because what she was going to do I thought was against the law, and also against God, but I said goodbye to her. Her friend and her boyfriend came to see the show and we had dinner together.

In the morning I phoned just to see how she was. The girl went in and when she came back she said, 'Miss Bronhill, I think she is dead. She's very cold.' It was goodbye to my Marianne.

4

In Love with London

In 1950, when I won the Sydney Sun Aria, the people of Broken Hill were absolutely ecstatic. They invited me back for great big civic receptions and it was all very grand. A couple of months later, a wonderful man in Broken Hill called Bill Welsh decided that he would start a fund to raise money to help me go to England because the prize money from the Aria competition was only £300. So they started having penny drives throughout the city. People would put down a penny, twopence, threepence, a threepenny bit, sixpence, a shilling or a two shilling piece, and at the end of the day they would collect all of this money and put it into the bank towards the fund.

They had concerts, they had parties – everything was a fund-raising effort to help June. The Zinc Mining Corporation, one of the big mining companies in Broken Hill, said that they would meet the fund pound for pound and then I did the most extraordinary thing – I got married to Brian Martin a year later, so the Zinc Corporation thought I was a bit of a risk and they didn't match it pound for pound. The townspeople eventually raised £1,500 for me which was a considerable amount of money in those days.

Brian and I sailed for London on the *Himalaya* in February 1952. I don't know when I've been more bored in my life than I was after about two weeks on board ship. I'm afraid I'm not really one who would ever again travel by sea. I didn't get seasick, but I was certainly very bored. You can only play so much deck tennis and quoits.

Also on board was a young Australian violinist, Beryl Kimber, and it soon got around that the *Himalya* was carrying two up and coming artistes, so consequently we were both asked if we would do a concert for the first class passengers and for the crew. Please note, not one for the second class passengers, which I thought was a bit rude, but I didn't have the cheek to say, 'Why can't we entertain our lot as well?' Beryl and I did a couple of concerts and we were very well received.

I remember as we were getting closer to England, about a fortnight out, I decided that, as we were going to poor war-starved, impoverished London, I would save all the pieces of fruit that came with my early morning cup of tea. I had this great big box that I'd obviously used to bring something on board with me, so I started keeping all these oranges, apples, pears and bananas. But imagine my surprise when we were on the boat train from Tilbury to London and the first thing that greeted my eyes as we travelled through Essex was these wonderful fruit shops stacked high with beautiful fruit and vegetables. Of course I left the mouldy old bits of fruit in the train when we got to St Pancras.

My dear aunt, uncle and cousin were there to meet us in London. Brian and I were going to stay with them. My aunt, Auntie Ida, was Dad's sister and it was just wonderful meeting her for the first time, having over all the years as a child in Broken Hill had letters and photographs from her and her family and then meeting them in the flesh. We went to Kenton, Harrow, where Brian and I stayed with them until we could find a flat of our own. We had lovely times talking about my father and his family, the Goughs, when they were young, with me catching up on things that I didn't know.

Even after throwing away all that mouldy fruit, we did arrive with some marvellous things in our trunks for the family – lovely great tins of ham, all sorts of things like sugar, flour and dried fruits which were not perishable, and we were greeted with open arms because at this time London was still on rationing – not only for food but for clothes. We, of course, had to line up and get our ration books, as we were going to be living in London, though we didn't know for how long.

Auntie Ida and Uncle Ernest took us exploring in London and we went on holiday together to Devon and Cornwall. At long weekends we used to venture somewhere else so that we could see more of England. Not only did I fall in love with London, but I also fell in love with England itself.

After a while it was time for me to start looking for Dino Borgioli, who was going to be my singing teacher, time for Brian to be getting a job and for us to be finding a flat. We eventually found one in Barnes, overlooking Barnes Common. It was in a great old corner house that was owned by the people who lived on the two floors beneath us – a lovely Jewish family called the Princes. Lesley, their son, was a London cabbie and he did a great job of teaching Brian about London, because Brian had now got himself a job with Berlei, the company he had worked for in Australia. Lesley helped me as well by showing me on the maps exactly how to direct Brian when I sometimes went with him on his calls as a representative.

Also I had found Dino Borgioli in Kensington. I had heard a recording in Australia of Borgioli singing some lovely *arie antique*, an English song called 'My Lovely Celia' and an American art song called 'Do Not Go, My Love', and these recordings made me decide that this was the man I wanted to study with. I had been told that he was teaching in London, so I'd made up my mind that there was nobody else that I could possibly study with but him.

I went and sang for him. He was very interested in me and said he would love to teach me. And so my singing lessons started. One of my lessons was the first lesson of the morning, at ten o'clock, and I had arrived there at about a quarter to ten. I suddenly heard Borgioli singing and I thought, 'I won't knock on the door, I'll just sit here and listen.' He was accompanying himself and singing some of these beautiful old Italians songs – *arie antique*. When the

40

June with Sir Joseph Post after winning the Sydney Sun Aria competition in 1950. Note the eyebrows!

June in 1950 in Sydney.

Madame Marianne Mathy, June's singing teacher in Sydney, around 1950.

Setting sail for England on the *Himalaya*, 1952. *Left to right:* Harry Constable, June, her husband Brian Martin, her sister Barbara and brother John.

The unknown soprano June Bronhill on the night of her first concert in London, a big charity concert at the Casino Theatre. This was in October 1953, before she joined Sadler's Wells.

June Bronhill as Leila with her leading man, tenor Charles Craig, in costume for *The Pearl Fishers* (1956).

time came for me to go in, I knocked on the door and went in, but I didn't let him know that I'd been sitting outside listening. His voice was still absolutely beautiful and gave me such joy that at the end of the lesson I said, 'Mr Borgioli, would it be all right if I had my lesson at this time every morning, because it would be much better for me as far as planning the rest of my day is concerned?' He said, 'Of course, perfectly all right, June.' Little did he know that my reason was that I was going to arrive every morning at half past nine and sit outside and listen to him do his warm-up! I learnt a lot from that as well as from my lessons.

He was a darling, gentle man and a gentleman. He reminded me incredibly of my father, with the same delicious sense of humour and warmth, and I think he sort of became my other Dad. He had a wonderful woman called Madame Amadio (or Amati) who was his accompanist. She was quite an elderly lady and she played the piano very well, but sometimes Dino would become frustrated with her because she wouldn't really follow his beating of the time of the music. He would say, 'Get away, you silly old woman, and I will play.' And, to my amazement, she always took it in very good part!

When I arrived in London, my voice wasn't in very good condition because towards the end of my studies with Madame Mathy, she had become too technical for me. A lot of her other students had found this as well. She would talk about things like 'lifting the larynx'. Well, I hadn't a clue how to lift my larynx, but sometimes I would do something – I don't know what – and she would say, 'Yes, that's right, darling.' I had started to yell a bit up around the top C area and my voice wasn't in the same good condition that it had been a year before. Consequently, when I went to Dino he said, 'Now we will start a serious period of training. You will not sing anything but exercises for six months.' I couldn't believe that I wasn't even going to be able to sing a little song, but that's what he said and that's what he meant! So for six months I did nothing but exercises—scales, arpeggios, legato, staccato, forte, pianissimo. Often he would put a belt around my waist and pull it very tightly, which gave tremendous support for the diaphragm. We worked and we worked and we worked and within about a month he had me scaling up to an A above top C, which is a very high note. As I say to lots of people, only the dogs can hear it! He said, 'For the coloratura voice you must scale higher. If I scale you to an A above top C, then you will have a good F above top C.' And he was perfectly right. Even today, when I do my exercises, while I don't need to have a top F any more, I do need to have an E flat above top C in my voice, so I scale up to an F and have a fairly solid E flat, certainly a very solid top D. I also still use the belt trick quite often!

It was a joy working with him, but it was quite wearing and I really got to the stage where I thought I'd never sing a song again. Then one day he said, 'Now we will start learning some beautiful songs and some arias.' We worked on the *arie antique*—lovely expressive songs which were beautiful to sing. And good for the voice! Also I started learning some operas, just certain passages. The first operatic role that I studied with him was that of Gilda in Verdi's *Rigoletto*. He sang every other role in the opera. It was really wonderful, though there were the times, of course, when he would push poor dear old Madame off the piano stool, saying, 'Get away, old woman, I'll play.' He was always smoking a cheroot, which was extraordinary, really, for a singing teacher. There was always a great packet of them on the piano. He also taught me the role of Violetta in the Verdi opera, *La Traviata*, and I worked on a lot of excerpts from Bellini's *La Sonnambula*. He taught me the true Italianate feeling of these operas and, even though I didn't speak any Italian (which I still don't, much to my disgust), — he taught me correct pronunication so that a lot of people really thought I did speak Italian because my pronunciation was so good. He was super to work with and I loved every minute of it.

Then, of course, after a while I was at him: 'When am I going to be allowed to audition for one of the opera companies?'

'Don't worry, I'll tell you when you're ready, I'll tell you when you're ready.'

I was lucky, of course, because having the money from Broken Hill meant that I didn't have to worry about getting work to pay for my lessons or having to ask Brian to help me. But I was becoming anxious and eventually, twenty months after I had been studying for him, he said that he felt I was ready to audition for the opera companies.

I sent off letters to Sadler's Wells and Covent Garden. Eventually I had an answer from Sadler's Wells asking me to audition for them. The first auditions were held in the Wells Room, a large room at the back of the dress circle where tea and coffee were served during intervals. This audition is with the chorus master and the chief repetiteur – the chief coach. I arrived in my little basic black number (we all auditioned in our basic black those days – just why, I've no idea!). I sang before Mr Marcus Dodds, the chorus master, and Mr Tom Hammond, the chief repetiteur.

At the end of my aria, Mr Dodds asked, 'Miss Bronhill, are you interested in chorus work?' I said, 'Oh, no way' in my best Australian accent. I did speak with quite a broad Australian accent in those days. He said, 'I had a feeling you wouldn't be. Now, if we can arrange for you to come and sing on stage for the general administrator, the general manager, the musical director and various members of the staff, would you be at all interested?' I said, 'Oh beauty, I'd love it, great.' Eventually I had another letter telling me my stage audition date and time. It was a Thursday afternoon in November 1953 and I remember it vividly.

The time was given as 4.15 so I was there in plenty of time – in the basic black dress once again – and I was called on to the stage. The auditorium was in darkness and I tried to see somebody sitting somewhere but couldn't see a soul. Eventually, from the back of the auditorium, I heard a disembodied voice say, in a terribly English accent, 'What are you going to sing for us, Miss Bronhill?' I put my hand up to shield my eyes so that I might be able to see someone but I couldn't see a thing. I replied, 'I'd like to sing the "Ciascun lo Dice" from *The Daughter of the Regiment* by Donizetti.'

The voice said, 'That will be splendid, Miss Bronhill.'

I said, 'OK,' went across and riffled through my music, found the aria, gave it to the accompanist, sang it and finished on an F above top C, one of those notes only the dogs can hear! They applauded me and I thought, 'Well, that can't be too bad!' I started picking up my music to walk off the stage when, suddenly, what had been a disembodied voice became the embodied voice of (as I found out later) the general administrator, Mr Norman Tucker. He came down the centre aisle to talk to me. He said, 'One moment, Miss Bronhill. We'd like to hear you sing something else. What do you have there?'

Once again, in my best Aussie accent, I said, 'I've got the "Ah! Fors'e Lui" from *La Traviata* by Verdi; I've also got the 'Caro Nome' from *Rigoletto*, which is also by Verdi [just in case he didn't know]; I've got a couple of Mozart arias and I've got the "Ah! Non Credea" and the "Ah! Non Giunge" from *La Sonnambula* by Bellini.'

He said, 'Oh, I think the Bellini will be splendid.'

'Right.' So I got the music out and as he started to go back up the aisle, I said, 'Oh, excuse me, sir, look, would you like it in Italian or English?'

He said, 'It doesn't really matter, Miss Bronhill,' to which I replied, 'That's just as well because I only know it in Italian!' I really did have the cheek of Old Riley!

I was delighted to hear that they wanted to offer me a contract. I arranged to go in and discuss it with Mr Tucker. It was agreed that I would be a principal soprano, starting in January 1954 at the ripe old salary of £10 per week, which I thought was marvellous. We had made a verbal agreement and when I got home from this meeting, there was a telegram from Covent Garden telling me not to sign anything with Sadler's Wells because they wanted to hear me sing. I got in touch with Covent Garden and said, 'I'll come along and sing for you, but I have given a verbal agreement to join Sadler's Wells.' They still wanted to hear me so I went along and sang for them, first in the foyer bar and then on stage. They seemed quite impressed and might have offered me a contract, but I said that there was nothing I could do because I had given Sadler's Wells a verbal agreement. So I missed out on Covent Garden but I was very happy to join Sadler's Wells.

When I look back on it, I realise that fate had turned me in the right direction because I know that if I had joined Covent Garden there would have been no *Merry Widow* for me and the *Widow* really set me on my terrific career. Also the principals at Covent Garden very rarely did any of the main roles – they generally did some of the minor roles, while most of the main roles were sung by visiting artists from America or the Continent. One of the few people really to get a great opportunity there of course was Joan Sutherland, with *Lucia di Lammermoor*.

I continued to work with Dino, lovingly, until I went home to Australia in 1960 with *The Merry Widow*. While I was there I heard the very sad news that he had died. I never did work with another singing teacher in London. I didn't feel that I could find anybody who could give me all the wonderful, instinctive tuition that Dino had given me. I have quite a few of his records and listen to them regularly. They are a great help. I will remember him for as long as I live. I loved him dearly.

5

Sadler's Wells' New Coloratura Soprano

When I joined Sadler's Wells in January 1954 I immediately started rehearsal for one opera and one operetta. My first performance was about four weeks later, when I played the role of Barbarina in *The Marriage of Figaro*. At the same time I was learning the lovely fun role of Adele in *Die Fledermaus*. One day I was rehearsing with Mr Hammond, the chief repetiteur, working on Adele's 'Laughing Song' with all its lovely coloratura trills, when suddenly there was a knock on the door. We stopped work and Mr Hammond said, 'Come in.' This young woman came in and he introduced her to me as Anna Pollak, one of their leading mezzo sopranos. He said, 'Oh, Anna, this is our new coloratura soprano, June Bronhill.' Anna raised her eyes to heaven and said, 'Oh God, not another nymphomaniac.' Tom laughed and I laughed. When Anna had gone I turned to Mr Hammond and said, 'Excuse me, Mr Hammond, but what's a nymphomaniac?' He explained what a nymphomaniac was and I was quite horrified, particularly as I had laughed so blithely! She probably went away with the impression that I was one. I was as naive as they come in those days.

The Rosalinda in that 1954 *Fledermaus* was one of the top sopranos of the company, Victoria Elliott, a wonderful-looking woman with a terrific voice but a real prima donna. Unfortunately, her diction wasn't all that good. In the second act, the ballroom scene, Rosalinda, who has discovered that her husband has gone to Prince Orlofsky's ball, when he really should have been going to prison, decides to disguise herself as a Hungarian countess. She arrives at the ball complete with a mask – the only person masked – and tells Prince Orlofsky that she is a Hungarian countess. The guests ask her to take off her mask. She says, 'No, I will not be unmasked.' Then eventually they say, 'If you are Hungarian, sing us an Hungarian song.' So she sings this wonderful *csardas* and while she's singing it, I was sitting on a chaise-longue with Prince Orlofsky, played by Anna Pollak, who had a delicious sense of humour. Halfway through the *csardas* Anna turned to me and said, 'I think she must be Hungarian – I can't understand a word she's singing.'

One of the productions already in performance when I joined the company was Donizetti's *Don Pasquale*. Halfway through my first few months at the Wells, the management told me that they wanted me to sing the role of Norina at the opening of the new season. At Sadlers Wells, we would work through until about middle or end of June and then have about six weeks' break, come back, rehearse for a few weeks and then start the new season in September. I was to open the season in September with Norina. I was very excited about this. Of course I told Dino the news and he was delighted. I explained to him that having seen the production a few times, I found that in the second act, where Norina is supposed to change from this sweet little Sophronia straight from the convent into a real little virago – and all hell should be let loose after she 'marries' Don Pasquale – she didn't have enough funny wicked things to do. She should absolutely tear the place apart, break things and really make Don Pasquale very upset. Dino told me the things that had happened when he used to play Ernesto, the tenor role in the opera. So when I started rehearsals I suggested that I would like to do a few more extraordinary things like break a few flowerpots, turn a few chairs over and fling papers all over the place. They said, 'Great, that's marvellous.' It made me very happy that I could have a bit more fun with it.

A lovely thing happened when the company was on tour. I was appearing in *Die Fledermaus* and learning the role of

Norina. The man coaching man me was a marvellous, absent-minded musician called David Andrews, a wonderful coach. We were in Nottingham and had done a session from ten till eleven, then we thought we'd have a coffee break. We went across the road to a Lyons Corner House. When we got there I said to David, 'I'll get these,' and he said, 'Oh, thank you; what do you want?' I told him I'd like a cup of coffee and a Bath bun, and he said, 'You sit down and I'll get them.' I gave him a ten-shilling note to pay for everything. I sat down waiting and suddenly David came along. He had a tray and on it were the things for himself, but nothing for me! He said, 'I'll see you afterwards at the rest of the rehearsal, June,' and walked past me and sat down somewhere else! I didn't have the courage to say anything to him! I had a very expensive morning coffee because then I had to get up and buy my own! It cost me about twelve shillings altogether! David was such a darling I didn't like to say anything, but it had completely gone from his head that I had given him the money.

My opening night as Norina was a great success. I had marvellous notices. I kept press cuttings for a long while but I never found time to put them in books so I can't really quote reviews. But I do remember one of the London critics likened me vocally to the great Lina Pagliughi. I was very honoured by that – I was quite thrilled, as a matter of fact!

Another press notice I had when I sang Gretel in Humperdinck's *Hansel and Gretel* is one of the few crits that I really do remember. In this opera, which Sadler's Wells had been presenting at Christmas for about five years, the Gretel was always sung by a delightful soubrette coloratura, Marian Studholme, and the Hansel was always Anna Pollak. They were the darlings of the audiences and everybody thought they were superlative in their roles. Suddenly one year the Wells decided they would change the casting. A charming mezzo soprano, Joyce Blackham, a wonderful singer and actress, was going to play Hansel and I was going to play Gretel. We thought we were pretty good but when one particular notice came out, we weren't quite so sure. Harold Rosenthal in *Opera* magazine got stuck into poor Joycey. He really tore her apart, saying she was just like a pantomime principal boy, that the show really wasn't the same, and how dreadfully they missed Anna Pollak and Marian Studholme. He added, 'All that could be said about June Bronhill as Gretel was that she was the right size for the part!'

One of my great memories of my Sadler's Wells days was when I was playing the role of Leila in *The Pearl Fishers* by Bizet. I'm very short — just under five feet — and in Leila's first scene she sings a wonderful incantation to the Gods to protect the pearl fishermen. I was surrounded by the leading males of the cast and naturally they were all considerably taller than me. At one performance one of them had been knocking back a few scotches before the show; another one, a Polish baritone, always had lots of garlic in everything he ate so his pores just reeked of garlic; and the other one had not the nicest breath! I had to stand in the middle of these gentlemen for about fifteen minutes while they sang over me. I don't know how I got through that particular night!

I was asked to sing the title role in *Martha*, a charming little opera by von Flotow. It really was lovely and I enjoyed singing it, particularly the interpolation of 'The Last Rose of Summer'. I was bowled over by a crit I got for this role. That critic said how well I had sung it and how beautifully I had acted it, but I shouldn't make it all look so easy. Now, what do you do about something like that?

I can't really remember what my feelings were when Sadler's Wells asked me if I would sing the Queen of Night's two arias from *The Magic Flute* for them on stage so that they could tell whether I could cope with the role. I hadn't really mastered the arias but I went on stage. Naturally I had to sing from the score. I handled the two arias reasonably well and they told me they wanted me to do the role in the new production. I accepted, and felt honoured and thrilled about it. However, it was during the rehearsals of *The Magic*

Flute that my husband had a nervous breakdown. Fitting in visits to him in hospital three times a day really was very exhausting for me because the Queen of Night is a fiendishly difficult role—one of the most difficult roles ever written, as only Mozart can write them! I was exhausted but luckily I had tremendous stamina (as I still have) and was able to cope.

Another incredible thing happened during the rehearsals of *The Magic Flute*. We had a wonderful European conductor, Rudolph Schwartz, and he had the most extraordinary beat. It was difficult to follow because the arms were not together. One day I was talking to one of the members of the orchestra and I said, 'You must tell me something—how on earth do you follow the maestro's beat?'

He said, 'June, the secret is that you don't look at his arms, you look at his mouth.'

'What do you mean?'

'You watch him—he goes pop, pop, pop, pop . . . pop . . . pop, pop, pop, . . . pop . . . pop and you get every note, every beat from the pop, pops.'

So after that I looked down and, sure enough, there were the pop, pops going. It was terribly easy to follow!

In *The Magic Flute*, I, as Queen of Night, and the Three Ladies wore extraordinary wigs, made of very thick wool which we used to call blanket wool. They were long and mine was black. I also had a wonderful glittery headdress. At one performance, before the second act aria (which is the most difficult of the two that the Queen of Night sings), there was a blackout and a flash of lightning and I suddenly appeared before my daughter, Pamina, played by an Australian soprano, Patricia Howard. To make my appearance I had to dash quickly between two raffia screens during the blackout. I did so and started my dialogue with Pamina, who looked at me and turned away. When she had to look at me for her dialogue lines she coped, but otherwise she was turning away and trying hard not to smile. I wondered what was the matter with her. Then I sang the aria, terrific applause, another blackout and flash of lightning and puff of smoke and off I dashed. I got into my dressing-room to discover that I had done the whole scene with my wig at a drunken skew-wiff angle! Obviously it had caught on the raffia as I'd come through and twisted right round. I really looked like a drunken Queen of Night. I hoped the audience hadn't noticed it – but they didn't laugh.

I had very good notices and a lot of people said that I was one of the best Queens of Night they'd ever seen, which was nice for me. The management wanted me to do some extra performances and by then I was just exhausted by coping with Brian's breakdown. Because of the difficulty of the role I thought it would be better for me to give up the role before the role gave me up. So I went to Mr Tucker in my own inimitable fashion – no appointment, I just knocked on the door. I said, 'Mr Tucker, I hope you don't mind but I would rather not do any more Queen of Nights.' He asked why and I explained. Then he said a marvellous thing: 'June, I wish more of the company would come to me and discuss things the way you do.' I'd been doing this kind of thing quite regularly. For instance, if I discovered that I didn't have any new roles coming up, or when the schedule came out and I didn't have a performance for six weeks, I'd just dive straight up to Mr Tucker and say, 'What's happening? Am I on the way out?' And he'd say, 'No. Wait until you see the next schedule and you'll be wishing that you had more free time.' I suppose it was just because of my Aussie upbringing and, once again, the cheek of Riley.

Part of the repertoire during the 1956–57 season was a programme of three one-act operas. The first one was *The Telephone* by Menotti, the second one was Bartók's *Bluebeard's Castle* and the third one was *Gianni Schicchi* by Puccini. I was asked to play Lucy in the curtain-raiser, *The Telephone*. This was the first time I had worked with Wendy Toye, who was directing, and Malcolm Pride, who was designing.

Malcolm designed the most divine set – it was terribly

modern, chrome furniture and quite angular, and everything was in pink and black. My dress was candy pink, I had a cute blonde wig rinsed with pink, and high-heeled pink satin shoes. Denis Dowling, a wonderful New Zealand baritone, was playing my boyfriend, Ben, and he was in a typical London business suit, black pinstripe trousers, black jacket and bowler. His grey hair had a pink rinse through it as well and he had a rolled umbrella, a black attaché case and a pink *Financial Times* under his arm. The dress that Malcolm designed for me was a wonderful confection of pink. It was like a little cocoon, a band of pink satin just below the knees and the rest was all pink chiffon gathered into the satin band. It was a real hobble skirt and with the high-heeled pink satin slippers I could just hobble along, but it was quite the most enchanting little dress and, would you believe, it started a fashion in London! The cocoon caught on quite rapidly.

As well as singing Lucy in *The Telephone*, I was understudying Lauretta in *Gianni Schicchi*. I hadn't had much rehearsal in it. At that time the man who was the general manager of Sadler's Wells Theatre, Doug Bailey, was also my agent. At this particular performance, Patricia Howard, who was singing Lauretta, said she didn't feel very well. It wasn't quite certain whether she would be going on that night or whether I would have to take over. I said it didn't matter, I'd just hang round and if Pat didn't want to go on at the last moment I'd keep my fingers crossed and I'd go on. Well, Pat didn't feel up to it so I went on. So Doug Bailey had to go out and make an announcement. He went on the stage and said, 'Owing to the indisposition of Miss Patricia Howard, the role of Lauretta will be sung by . . .' and he blanked. He looked into the wings and the stage management weren't in the wings, they were doing other things, and Doug said, 'Will be sung by . . .' He was panicking because even though he knew me so well he couldn't think of my name. Eventually he was clicking his fingers into the wings and there came 'June Bronhill'. He said, 'Oh yes, will be sung by Miss June Bronhill.' Even when they know you, they don't know you!

Working with Wendy on the *The Telephone* was a joy because this was the first time that I had worked with a director who had been a ballet dancer and choreographer. She taught me so much about deportment. She was always saying to me, 'June darling, shoulders back and down. You will elevate yourself and you'll look inches taller.' I'm eternally grateful to Wendy, because it's amazing the number of people who meet me these days after a performance who don't know me and say, 'But you're so short. On stage you look inches taller!' That's Wendy Toye — she's a marvellous teacher.

Sadler's Wells decided to do John Gardner's opera, *The Moon and Sixpence*, which was based on the novel by Somerset Maugham. Most people feel that this was based on Gauguin. One of the highlights of this production was the lighting. In one act, the setting is Tahiti, on the beach with a tropical landscape outside his thatched hut. Sitting in the audience, as I did one day during a final dress rehearsal, you could feel that heat radiating from the stage — it was the most extraordinary feeling and reaction. We had a wonderful lighting man called Charlie Bristow who could achieve extraordinary effects. This, I think, was one of his greatest, because you really wanted to get a fan and start fanning yourself.

In 1961 I was asked to do the two prestigious new productions of the season. The first one was the title role of the Vixen in Janáček's *The Cunning Little Vixen*. It was wonderfully directed by Colin Graham and I just loved doing it. You had to forget everything you had ever done on stage before because you had to move and think like an animal. You couldn't stand completely straight, you had to be slightly stooped, so that you had the look of an animal on the prowl and all the time, that look of awareness, of sniffing for danger, of being on the alert. I learnt so much from doing that opera, and I loved working with Colin Graham, who taught me so much.

The other production of that 1961 season was Richard Strauss's *Ariadne auf Naxos* in which I played Zerbinetta —

a wonderful role, a great acting part, with one of the most difficult arias to sing in the second act. Anthony Besch was the director and he had me doing some unreal things for an opera singer, quite balletic things. In the fiendish aria, I was trilling away, doing terrific vocal gymnastics, when the boys—one on either side—had to pick me up in a fully balletic hold and, with their help, I had to leap over the other boys and land, boom, directly behind the footlights. It was unbelievable, quite extraordinary, and yet I did it! He even had me pirouetting, little old me. Anthony Besch was a miracle worker.

I was asked to play the role of Lucinda in the comic opera, *The School for Fathers*, by Wolf-Ferrari. When the company had done the production originally, it appears that one night, during a performance, Sadler, the company's cat, just strolled on to the stage and wandered around. This was in the garden scene. Sadler went up to the rubbish bin at the back, nosed around in it, then jumped up on the wall and sat there until the curtain came down. Well, it caused such a sensation that they decided to see if Sadler would do it at every performance. Sadler duly obliged, which was wonderful. But when we came to our production, Sadler has disappeared—nobody knew what happened to him and it was a great loss to everybody. The management decided to have auditions for a cat. Well, I must tell you the place was in chaos, utter chaos! It was like stage mums and their children, but instead they were coming in to audition their pet cats. The press coverage was fantastic! A cat was eventually chosen. The creature was quite incredible—it did the same thing every performance. It would come on, look around, then jump straight up on the back wall and sit there with its back to the audience and its tail swishing backwards and forwards in time to the music. That's all it did and of course it brought the house down. We might just as well not have been on stage.

During the last week of rehearsals I developed a dreadful bronchitis. I couldn't go to the dress rehearsals because I was so ill. For some extraordinary reason I didn't have an understudy. The girl who had originally played my part was playing another part and they hadn't bothered to get somebody to learn my part. Consequently, because of the hullaballoo that had gone on with the auditions of the cat, I thought I had to go on, I had to keep the curtain up. So I went on and battled through – it's a very difficult role to sing. I just made it, only to receive dreadful press notices. I hadn't had an announcement made to say that I was suffering badly and the press said some really terrible things about me. The consequence of it all was that I damaged my voice so badly that it took me a good six weeks to two months before it got back into shape again. I always say these days that I do not believe anybody should keep the curtain up if they're going to do themselves any damage, either vocally or as far as the press is concerned, and unless I am positive that I can give a performance worthy of an audience who has paid money to hear and see a good performance, I'm not going to perform and go by that old saying, 'the show must go on'. I do not see why the performer should suffer.

I was asked to play the role of Blonde in Mozart's *Il Seraglio*, a role I had played years before in Australia. I remember at one performance, when I was singing Blonde's second aria, a very cheeky little piece, and bouncing all over the stage while singing it, jumping up and down steps, I suddenly became aware of strange gestures in the pit from Colin Davis, the conductor. I couldn't work out what I was doing incorrectly. I kept looking down, and there he was, still making these funny gestures. I didn't know whether I was singing in the wrong place so I listened carefully, but no, I was with the music, and I was doing all the right Mozart dynamics. I started to get dreadfully frustrated. I was almost at the stage where I could quite cheerfully have stopped and said, 'Mr Davis, do you think you could tell me what I'm doing wrong so that I can get it right which will obviously make you happier.' But I thought, 'No, battle on, June, battle on.' So I battled on. At the end of the performance, after we'd taken our curtain calls and we were all walking off the stage, I went to Mr Davis and said, 'Mr Davis, what was I doing wrong in my second aria?'

'What do you mean, what were you doing wrong?'

'Well, you were doing all sorts of strange hand gestures to me and I couldn't work out what I was doing incorrectly.'

'Oh no, June, it wasn't you, you were absolutely fine. It was one of the woodwind players. He was doing all sorts of dreadful things and I just couldn't catch his eye!'

So I felt a little happier after that.

Interspersed with all of these roles were lots of other terrific roles that I played for the company and I enjoyed my term with Sadler's Wells enormously. I was a member of the company from January 1954 to August 1961. I did go back later to do Saffi in *The Gypsy Baron* in 1964 and in 1972 to do *The Merry Widow* again.

Before we started production rehearsals of *The Gypsy Baron* we had a meeting with the director and the designer. The designer was an Arab gentleman who told us he had designed these very simple sets, just rocks and things, so there was a lot of space for everyone to move, particularly in the big gypsy scenes. But when it came to actually doing the production with these sets, it turned out that the rocks were constructed of papier mâché, so you couldn't stand on them. You had to walk around them and consequently the people were standing in great clumps because the rocks took up so much room.

In *The Gypsy Baron*, I had a marvellous scene with a wonderful mezzo soprano, Anne Howard, singing Czipra, and Nigel Douglas, a super tenor, singing Barinkay. Czipra tells us she has dreamt where the gold is hidden and Barinkay and Saffi sit down and listen to this marvellous aria. I was instructed to sit on one of these rocks. At one performance I sat there quite happily. My costume had a loose mesh belt around it and when I got up to ask where the gold was, there was this great big boulder dangling from my sash, just bouncing round like a feather. I tried to get it off but couldn't.

Eventually, with help from Nigel, it came off. It was hysterical and the audience fell about laughing. We three on stage could hardly keep a straight face either, as you can well imagine.

When we first started rehearsals on stage with the sets, the place where the gold was to come from really did look like the biggest phallic symbol imaginable and when Czipra pressed a particular stone, the gold started rushing out of this thing so you can imagine what it looked like! We complained to the director and said it was just too dreadful for words; the audience would shriek with laughter when they saw it. So they decided to put a few bullrushes around it and you can imagine what they looked like as well, can't you! On opening night, when the gold poured out of this thing, the audience just creased into laughter. It was like that every performance and we never knew where to put ourselves.

6

The Merry Widow

In 1955 Sadler's Wells decided to do a production of Franz Lehar's *The Merry Widow*. Lots of purists in the company thought it was a bad thing for the Wells to degrade themselves by doing such a thing, thinking, of course, of the musical comedy version, not the original operetta version. Personally, I was not in the least anxious about the whole thing because I didn't for one moment think that I would be chosen to play the title role. Lots of other sopranos in the company were at each other's throats; they were all very excited about the possibility of playing the role of the Widow, whereas I had always thought of the Widow as being rather tall, elegant and sophisticated. Those of you who know me know that I'm certainly not tall, elegant and sophisticated! However, Charles Hickman, the director, had seen me as Norina in *Don Pasquale*, a lovely frivolous soprano role, and as he had decided that he wanted his Merry Widow to be the soubrette type rather than the elegant, sophisticated type, he decided that I was to be his Merry Widow. The other sopranos were furious and I was shattered. I was going to be saddled with that song 'Vilja' again! I had been singing it *ad nauseum*, as you know, from childhood until I was about seventeen, and here I was, stuck with it again. But I soon discovered that I loved that Widow lady very much. She was really delightful.

Rehearsals proceeded and it was coming along marvellously. Then, suddenly, the blow came. We had to shelve our *Merry Widow* because of a big court case between the Lehar Estate and a company which had involvements with *The Merry Widow*, over the copyright. Then, in November 1957, it was announced that everything had been settled and we could go ahead with our production.

We rehearsed like crazy. I can tell you I'd never rehearsed like that before in my life. We would work from ten in the morning until one without a break. Charles Hickman was one of those directors (like me as a performer) who doesn't like a break in the middle of a rehearsal session, as it always takes a while to get back into the swing of things. (This, of course, was when we were rehearsing without the chorus, because with the chorus you had to break because of the Equity rules.) Then we would have a lunch break from one until two, and then work non-stop from two until five. Tom Round and I would have half an hour's break and then we'd work from half past five until seven o'clock on the famous *Merry Widow* waltz.

Charles Hickmam was absolutely wonderful to work with, but once he'd blocked everything, and worked out all our moves, he would then start his incredible habit of just watching us, not saying anything, just watching and chewing handkerchiefs! He must have gone through about three or four handkerchiefs a day, just chewing, chewing, chewing, and then suddenly the handkerchief would be thrown away and, boom, he would start! 'So , why haven't you been doing so and so? Why don't you do this? Let's think about this again,' and so on. He got through so many handkerchiefs that my first night present to him was always dozens of beautiful hand-rolled Swiss cotton handkerchiefs. God only knows how long they lasted!

It was all absolutely exhausting, but incredibly exciting and stimulating. I even started to like 'Vilja' again, which was a good thing, because it seems that I am going to be stuck with it for the rest of my life!

One of the things about this production was that we *had* to be a success because Sadler's Wells was literally on the brink of closing down. *The Merry Widow*, we hoped, would bring a lot of people back into the theatre and bring in a new audience to see operas that they'd perhaps been a little afraid of seeing before. The sets were lovely, very simple, and literally done on a shoe-string, but wonderfully inventive. My costumes were beautiful, both to look at and to wear. I don't think I've ever loved costumes as much as I loved my original *Merry Widow* ones. I was tiny in those days, very slim, and I really looked pretty good!

Opening night – 28 January 1958 – eventually arrived. The excitement generated in my dressing-room over the Tannoy system as I sat making-up and the audience milled into the theatre was quite electrifying. Eventually I was called for my entrance. I was shaking like a leaf, and that awful thing happened that happens to so many of us when we are nervous and we know that a lot depends on the success of that night – my mouth became as dry as a bone! No matter how much water I sipped, it didn't make any difference. Suddenly, all the chorus men were calling, 'The widow, the widow, the merry widow! Twenty million francs!' and there was no turning back! All the men lined up on the staircase to receive me and I made my entrance. Then something happened that I wasn't expecting – the whole theatre erupted into a mammoth round of applause! I could barely hear the orchestra. Luckily the conductor, marvellous Alexander Gibson, threw my cue at me and I got it. Eventually the audience quietened down and we all knew from that moment that we'd done it, we'd really made a hit.

There was one hitch in that opening performance. When Danilo (Tom Round) came over to me with his arm outstretched to twirl me into his arms for the waltz we'd worked so hard on, he said, 'I can't turn my back on the audience. I've just split my trousers!' It was a scream because we had to improvise. We got by, but it was nothing like the marvellous waltz Pauline Grant had choreographed for us. After the performance Pauline said, 'What have I done to you that you should spoil my beautiful waltz so much? I just stood at the back of the circle and I couldn't believe what you were doing!'

Tom said, 'I'm sorry, Pauline, but as I bent down, just before the waltz, I split my trousers, so I went over to June and told her, and we just had to make it up.'

Pauline laughed and said, 'I thought it couldn't have been something I'd ever done to you!'

The night was quite the most wonderful night imaginable. When I sang 'Vilja' the audience went absolutely wild and I had to do an encore. Charles Hickman had anticipated this and had come up with this marvellous idea of blacking out the stage and putting a pin spot on my head. I had on a pretty tinkling head-dress which glittered with crystals, gold and sequins, and looked fantastic in the tiny spotlight. I sang the encore in the softest of voices and, once again, the audience went wild. I thought, 'Well, it can't be bad, all of this, can it?'

The end of the night was terrific. I had never known anything like it. The audience was ecstatic, oceans of flowers arrived on stage and everybody was so thrilled. We had done it! By the time I got back to my dressing-room I was almost in tears from all the excitement.

There was a message to say that Evelyn Laye was in the audience. She had played the Merry Widow many years before in the musical comedy version and she was longing to come around and meet me. That was the beginning of a very dear friendship. She was in tears, I was in tears and the press were taking photographs of us. Miss Laye showed me a beautiful Franz Lehar medallion she was wearing which had been given to her by Lehar when she sang the Widow.

Pauline Grant's sleeve notes for our EMI recording of *The Merry Widow* say:

On the 28th January, 1958, Sadler's Wells Theatre enjoyed one of those rare occasions which renews the faith of the already converted, and enthralls scores of initiates into lifelong subjection to the magic, mystery and tyranny of Theatre.

Spontaneous and prolonged explosions of applause hailed the return of Lehar's ubiquitous 'Widow' to the London scene she had first captivated fifty-one years before.

As the excitement increased throughout the evening it became apparent that not only was she adding another triumph to her already impressive career, but was bringing heart-warming rewards to every single factor concerned in her re-appearance – particularly the adventurousness of the Sadler's Wells management, the sensitive musical direction of Alexander Gibson and to Charles Hickman's suave, sparkling and inventive staging.

In the foyers, during the intervals, controversial opinions about the newest 'Widow' – June Bronhill – abounded amongst those treasuring nostalgic memories of her predecessors; but those of us meeting this capricious vision for the first time were entirely fascinated by June's glimmering, effortless vocal tone and her vital but unaffected interpretation.

It was a magnificent night, but the best thing about it was that we'd put Sadler's Wells back on its feet! The thing we had all hoped for happened – many people who had come to see the operetta version of *The Merry Widow* and had never seen an operetta before decided it wasn't all that bad after all and they came to see other operas, ones we call 'pot-boilers', like *La Bohème, Madame Butterfly, Tosca* and *La Traviata*. We did build up a new audience and Sadler's Wells got a new lease of life.

In April and May we went on the spring tour. As the *Widow* was such a success, we did at least four or five performances of it a week – out of six performances a week, that is! Everywhere we went, once again we had a tremendous success and there wasn't a performance where I didn't have to do that enchanting encore of 'Vilja'.

At this stage of the game, my Sadler's Wells salary was £18 a week – not much really for four or five performances a week of a leading role! On top of that I was getting £4 10s a week touring allowance, total £22 10s a week. That was fine until I discovered that Buddy Jones, a member of the chorus, who was playing the non-singing role of the secretary, Negus, was getting £13 a week salary and £5 week touring allowance. (Why choristers got a bigger touring allowance than principals I just don't know!) On top of that, for each performance of a main role, choristers got an extra three guineas. That meant that when we were doing five shows a week, Buddy Jones was getting fifteen guineas on top of his £13, which made £28 15s, plus his touring allowance of £5, which all added up to £33 15s. There was I, playing the Widow, getting a total of only £22 10s a week! God, how we laughed!

When we got back from the tour I went to see the general manager, Mr Stephen Arlen, and told him what I had found out about what Buddy was getting. Mr Arlen fell about laughing and I immediately got a rise of £4 10s a week. Big deal! But I had won my point and the whole thing was quite a shriek.

One exciting result of the great success we had with the *Widow* was that we were asked to take it to the Coliseum, one of London's largest commercial theatres which seats about 2,300 people. It was amazing to see how the set transferred from the rather small stage at Sadler's Wells to the enormous Coliseum stage. We had a fabulous success there. We broke all box office records, which was a great thrill, and we were immediately asked to return the following year – 1959 – for a six-month season. It was decided that we would do the *Widow* again, of course, and two new productions, Strauss' *Die Fledermaus* and another Lehar operetta, *The Land of Smiles*.

In *The Land of Smiles* I was to play Princess Mi who was the sister of Prince Sou-Chong, sung and performed magnificently by Charles Craig. I was doing all the performances of Princess Mi and I was doing all the Merry Widows. I was sharing the role of Adele in *Die Fledermaus* with the lovely Marion Studholme. The company offered me a £100 week for the season, which I suppose was pretty good for those days, but I thought that because of all the work involved (seven performances a week, most weeks) I should get more. I decided I wanted £175 a week.

One day after a morning rehearsal at the Wells, when I was going into the pit bar at the back of the stalls, Stephen Arlen was ahead of me in the queue. I told him that I didn't think my money for the Coliseum season was enough.

'Well, how much do you want?' he asked.

Bold as brass, I said, 'A hundred and seventy-five pounds.'

After he'd picked himself up from the floor, he said, 'Oh, June, we couldn't possibly pay that. We just can't afford it; the most we could go to is a hundred and twenty, or perhaps a hundred and twenty-five.'

To which I answered, 'Look, I'll tell you what, Mr Arlen. We'll toss a coin. If it comes down heads, you give me my hundred and seventy-five and if it comes down tails I'll accept your original offer of a hundred.'

He was floored. He said, 'June, if you are willing to gamble like that, you can have your hundred and seventy-five.'

A bit cheeky, wasn't I? It worked, though!

Die Fledermaus was the first production to go on and it had the most divine sets you've ever seen, with revolving staircases, the lot. It was directed by Wendy Toye and the whole production bubbled like champagne. It was really quite beautiful. Then came *The Land of Smiles*. My dear Charles Hickman directed this with great style and charm. Once again we had stunning sets and costumes, and the whole effect was too beautiful for words. I was sitting in the auditorium at the Coliseum one day when we were doing a dress rehearsal and I said to the person sitting with me, 'If this doesn't have the same success as the *Widow* had, I'll eat my hat!' It's just as well nobody took me up on that, because, strangely enough, it wasn't the success that we expected. I think people still had in their minds the production many years before in which Richard Tauber sang Prince Sou-Chong. They had worshipped Tauber. But even so it was an incredible season. It was wonderful to work in that great theatre for six months. The Coliseum eventually became the new home of the Sadler's Wells Opera Company or, as it is called today, the English National Opera.

Our next operetta was to be the sparkling *Orpheus in the Underworld* by Offenbach. We had a fantastic production team: Wendy Toye was directing; Alexander Faris (or Sandy, as he is known) was our musical director, and what Sandy doesn't know about Offenbach isn't worth worrying about; and we had a clever and inventive designer, Malcolm Pride. The main principals were some of Sadler's Wells' best known comedy people. Calliope was played brilliantly by Anna Pollak. Two fellow Australians, John Weaving, a handsome tenor, and Kevin Miller, a delightful lyric tenor, played the wicked Pluto and Orpheus respectively. Eric Shilling, a wonderfully funny man with a marvellous baritone voice, played Jupiter, with the one and only Sheila Rex as Juno. We also had the lovely Suzanne Steele as the sexiest Diana you've ever seen anywhere, and I was Eurydice.

It was the most stunning production, inventive and amusing, and had the most enormous success imaginable. The costumes were quite magnificent, and great fun. In some of mine I felt that I was pretty bare, particularly in a bubble bath costume, which I had to wear in a duet with Eric Shilling (Jupiter) in which he had disguised himself as a Golden Godfly and was flirting with Eurydice. This costume was a flesh-coloured, skin-tight leotard, cut very low at the back and front, and trimmed with long strips of tuille. On these and the leotard were sewn lots of plastic bubbles, so that when I was walking it looked as though I had nothing on but lots of soap bubbles! I'll never forget the first day I had to wear it on stage. It was an orchestral rehearsal and I felt so embarrassed in this naked-looking costume, but I felt quite a bit better when some of the fellows in the orchestra gave me a wolf whistle!

A funny thing happened in a performance of *Orpheus* a few years later in Australia. A lovely Australian tenor called David Gray was playing Orpheus. In a scene with Eurydice and Orpheus, on stage there were three busts of composers – Bach, Offenbach and Beethoven – on plinths. Inside the plinths were three of the ballet dancers who had been shepherds in the first scene and they had to walk inside the busts. There came a point where they had to turn around and go offstage. At one matinee the first two got off well but we could suddenly see that the third one was tottering—he'd caught his foot in the floor cloth! He was desperately trying to hold himself up but down it crashed. While David Gray and I were singing away we could see this figure trying desperately to lever the thing back on its feet, which, of course, was impossible. For about five minutes he struggled, while the audience shrieked with laughter, and David and I didn't quite know how to cope. Suddenly we saw little feet, then legs, then a body dressed as a shepherd, come out, pick up the plinth, look at the audience and rush off, carrying the plinth and the bust. David and I were in hysterics, the audience were falling about, and the orchestra were up on their feet looking at what was going on but still playing. We couldn't hear the orchestra for the laughter. Eventually I looked down at the conductor and said, 'I don't know where I am. Give me a clue and a cue! Somehow we managed to get it all back on its feet—pardon the pun!

During rehearsals of the Wells production of *Orpheus* the exciting news had come that Garnet Carroll, a marvellous entrepreneur in Australia, and David N. Martin, of the Tivoli Circuit, were negotiating to bring *The Merry Widow* to Australia. Of course, I was thrilled beyond belief that I would be going home to Australia for the first time in eight and a half years.

We arrived in Australia towards the end of June 1960. The press was out in full force, and the excitement that was generated was incredible. We didn't have our original Danilo, Tom Round, with us as unfortunately he had to do other operas for Sadler's Wells. However, we had instead a wonderful young tenor from the company called John Larsen, who instantly became a matinee idol. He was a tall, broad-shouldered, good-looking blond who always looked very dashing. The women just absolutely flocked after him.

We opened in Melbourne at the Tivoli Theatre and we played for eleven weeks to absolute capacity houses. I was told that at matinees they were even paying twelve and sixpence to stand, which was quite unheard of in those days.

We then moved up to Sydney where we did a nine-week season and once again it was the same, packed to capacity, and people paid exorbitant amounts to stand. It was a great success both artistically and financially for the entrepreneurs and for Sadler's Wells coming to Australia for the first time, and it was a great success for me too! Or perhaps I should say a great success for me on the whole, because I heard two funny stories which could have showed that not everyone was equally impressed.

At a matinee performance in Melbourne the place was jammed. Before the Widow's entrance there was all this kerfuffle: 'It's the Merry Widow, she's arrived, the Merry Widow,' etc., and they all want to get at her because she's got twenty million francs. Then I appeared, there was terrific applause from the audience, I came down the front, the applause stopped and I started singing the wonderful entrance of the Merry Widow. At the end of the song there was incredible applause. The company director was standing at the back of the circle and he heard a little old lady turn to someone and say, 'I think that must be June Bronhill.'

One day a fellow member of the cast was in a post office. He happened to hear these two ladies talking to each other. One said, 'I went to see *The Merry Widow* last night, with June Bronhill.'

And the other one said, 'Did you enjoy it?'

'Oh, yes, it was lovely. But I'll tell you this much, my Auntie Wynne sings "Vilja" just as well as she does, if not better.'

But I don't let that sort of thing spoil the season for me!

In one performance I had come on stage at the beginning of the second act, which is where the Widow sings 'Vilja', gone through the first verse and chorus, then moved across in the break music to the other side of the stage and sat down on a bench in the garden. I started to sing the second verse and I sang, 'She welcomed the huntsman with . . .' and I hadn't a clue what she welcomed him with. It should have been 'white lily hand' but it would not come into my mind.

Everyone around me, chorus and principals, were whispering the words to me but I couldn't take them in at all. As I've said, I have pretty good diction, so if ever I forget a word it's the most obvious thing in the world. Then, almost like a miracle, I saw in front of me the old sheet copy which someone had given me when I was eleven with the old words, and I just started singing them. Afterwards all the kids came up to me and said, 'June, they were marvellous, those words you made up.' I said, 'I couldn't make up anything—I saw my old sheet copy of the old words and that's what I sang— the words from the old musical comedy version.' But, if somebody had asked me to sing those words before I went on, I wouldn't have been able to because they had been completely erased from my mind by our new Sadler's Wells' Christopher Hassell version.

Garnet Carroll asked me if I'd come back the following year and do *The Sound Of Music* for him, but I'll tell you all about that later. In December, in the middle of an unbelievably hot summer, we flew back to London and arrived to bitterly cold, typically English winter weather. I had to go straight from London to Stratford-upon-Avon where I was to do a revival of *Orpheus in the Underworld* over the Christmas/New year period.

Something happened to me during that period that had never happened before and has never happened since, thank heavens. At the same time as I was preparing for *Orpheus* in Stratford, I was also working on the difficult role of Zerbinetta in *Ariadne auf Naxos* and learning another operetta by Offenbach, *La Vie Parisienne*. Just what happened, I don't know. I think I must have been under a tremendous physical and mental pressure from the workload as well as coming from the heat of Australia to the bitterly cold weather in England, and everything took its toll of me.

I was getting ready for the Saturday afternoon matinee of *Orpheus in the Underworld* when suddenly I just started shaking all over. I've never known anything like it. I was shaking and shivering, then I started crying. I asked my dresser to get the stage manager for me and I just said to him, 'I can't go on.' I was just like a piece of jelly, shaking and shaking. As it happened, my cover-understudy wasn't in Stratford for some extraordinary reason. So they asked that famous question, 'Is there a doctor in the house?' and there was. A doctor came around to see me and he told the company manager that I couldn't possibly go on. He felt I was at the beginning of a nervous breakdown and I should be taken back to London straightaway. I lay there shivering, shaking and crying, and I heard the announcement over the Tannoy that the performance had to be cancelled owing to my indisposition and if the public cared to go the the box office, they would have their money refunded. It was an absolutely packed house at the Royal Shakespeare Memorial Theatre and I couldn't have cared less! It was the most terrible sensation – I couldn't care less.

We were supposed to be doing *Orpheus* again that night but the company had also been rehearsing *Merry England* which was due to open the following week, so they had to put that on for the evening performance, not completely rehearsed but it did keep the curtain up. My cover-understudy was there to do *Orpheus* on Monday.

I was taken straight back to London where my friends contacted my doctor, a marvellous doctor who is a consultant surgeon, Mr Edward McLellan. Mac came to see me and said, yes, I was definitely on the verge of a nervous breakdown and if I wanted to give into it, I could go ahead and have a nervous breakdown, but if I did exactly what he prescribed, gave myself a week's complete rest and took the tablets he prescribed, I would be right there, back on my feet again. So I did as I was told and Mac was right. In ten days I was doing an orchestral rehearsal of *Ariadne auf Naxos*. No nervous breakdowns for Bronhill!

So having got over all that and back into the performances of *Orpheus in the Underworld*, we then started rehearsals for *La Vie parisienne*. We had exactly the same team as for *Orpheus* – Wendy Toye as director, Sandy Faris

69

as conductor, Malcolm Pride as designer, Anna Pollak, John Weaving, Kevin Miller, Eric Shilling, Suzanne Steele and Bronhill. This was a gem of a production, hilariously funny and absolutely beautiful to look at. I've had some beautiful costumes to wear but these were quite something else. There were so many different facets to my role of Gabrielle and, consequently, so many costume changes that it was like a never-ending fashion parade. It was as much fun as *Orpheus* and once again it was a tremendous success. We packed them in everywhere we went.

This was the time when I was christened Queen of Operetta because I seemed to be doing all the operettas put on by the Wells!

7

Lucia, Gilda and Yum Yum

Towards the end of 1958 when I was very busy with my *Merry Widow*s, I had a telephone call from Covent Garden asking me if I would be interested in understudying Joan Sutherland as Lucia di Lammermoor. Naturally I jumped at it. I didn't think I'd ever get a chance to play the role, of course, but I thought I'd love to be part of it because I knew that Franco Zeffirelli was directing the opera and I was excited at the prospect of watching him work, apart from learning the role. So I said yes. I actually learnt the role in Italian ten days, which I thought was pretty good.

I started attending all the rehearsals and was fascinated to see how Zeffirelli worked – it was an object lesson, the whole thing. The things he made Joan do were quite miraculous, although there were many times when she'd say, 'Oh, Franco, I can't do that, I feel so silly.' Joan didn't have that natural acting flair that, say, Callas had and that I believe I have developed over the years. But he got her to do some wonderful things. I gleaned everything I could from listening to his directions and watching him act out things the way he wanted them performed.

One day at the first dress rehearsal on stage at the Royal Opera House, Covent Garden, I was sitting in the auditorium watching when suddenly I realised that somebody was sitting behind me. It was Lord Harewood. He asked me, 'Would you like to do some performances?'

'What a stupid question! Of course I would.'

'There are a few that Joan can't do and we just thought it would be lovely to give you an opportunity.'

I just grabbed at it and I did five performances for them. At my first orchestral rehearsal, after I had finished singing the whole opera, the orchestra gave me a wonderful round of applause, which was a great thrill for me. I thought it was absolutely marvellous and even more marvellous when later somebody told me that the orchestra had only done that three times for any soprano, ever. One was Mattiwilda Dobbs in *Le Coq d'Or*; the second was when Joan had her first orchestral rehearsal of *Lucia di Lammermoor* and I was the third! I felt very honoured.

I had one rehearsal in costume on stage and, of course, the costumes had been designed for Joan who was quite a big lady and in those days I was incredibly tiny. Hence I found the materials, which were heavy plaids and lush silks on heavy crinoline underskirts, were very heavy indeed to wear. At that rehearsal, while I was going up the stairs backstage to make an entrance before the wedding scene, a press photographer standing nearby saw that I was having difficulty getting up the steps. He asked me, 'Are the steps too steep?' I said, 'No, legs too short,' and that made the *Evening Standard*!

I revelled in playing the role and I certainly felt that I had put a lot of what Zeffirelli wanted into the role. Sometime later a friend told me that a psychiatrist had told him that he had seen my performances at Covent Garden and he thought that in the mad scene I was a perfect example of a schizophrenic!

At that time I was doubling: one night I was doing *Lucia di Lammermoor* at Covent Garden and the next night I'd be singing *The Merry Widow* at Sadler's Wells. I don't think there are many sopranos around today that have done that, or want to do it, or could do it! My press notices in general were good ones. Some of them, naturally, compared me to Joan Sutherland and said that I was not dramatic enough for the role, but I didn't see Lucia that way. I saw her as a young girl who gradually went mad because she thought she'd been betrayed by the man she loved. But one of the press notices, by Andrew Porter in the *Financial Times*, was headed 'Not one Lucia, but Two — and They're Both

As Lucy in the Sadler's Wells production of Menotti's *The Telephone* (1957).

In the title role of von Flotow's opera, *Martha* (1957).
June's first *Merry Widow*, the Sadler's Wells production of
1958.

On the opening night of *The Merry Widow* June met Evelyn Laye, a former Merry Widow, backstage after the show.

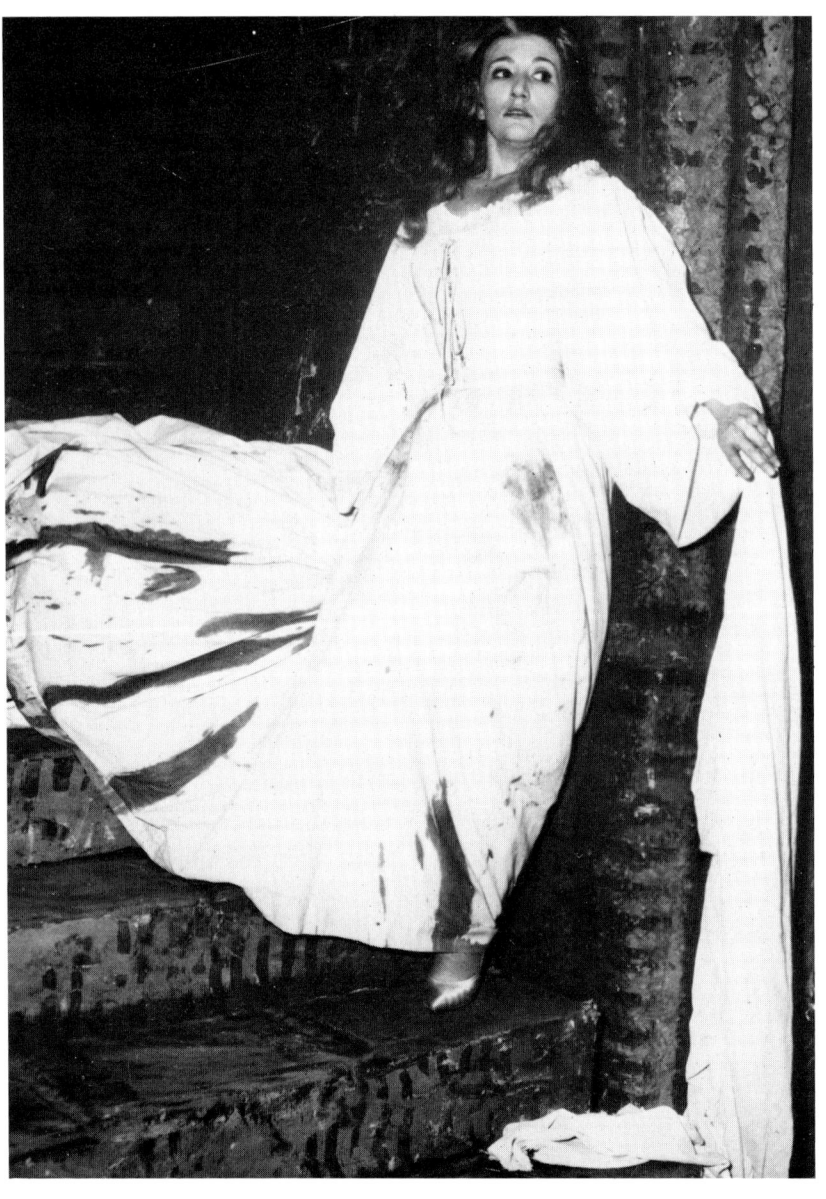

June as Lucia in the Mad Scene of *Lucia di Lammermoor*. June sang at several performances, as well as understudying Joan Sutherland, for the 1959 Covent Garden production.

Australian'. I thought that was pretty good for Australia!

Apart from my initial season with the NSW National Opera Company way back in 1951 before I went to England, the first opera I ever did in Australia was with the Elizabethan Theatre Trust Opera Company, which was the forerunner of the Australian Opera Company. For this company I did *Don Pasquale* in which I played Norina, of course, and Adele in *Die Fledermaus*. The *Don Pasquale* was really quite a charming production, done on a revolving stage. We did it in Sydney, Melbourne and Adelaide and then later in that year, which was 1967, we did a country tour. It was part of the policy of the Elizabethan Theatre Trust Opera Company to do country tours of New South Wales. Most of the company travelled in a bus but I travelled everywhere with Richard, my second husband, in our white Mark 10 Jaguar – proper posh! One of the marvellous things about *Don Pasquale* is that there are only two chorus numbers in the whole of the opera and these can be cut easily, which means that on tour you need only take away your principal singers. Naturally we didn't tour an orchestra, just a pianist, playing and conducting from the pit, and of course a small stage crew. Altogether we were just a little company of about eighteen people. We had a marvellous time. It was a tremendous success everywhere we went, all over the state, even out to Broken Hill, where we did four performances.

We flew to Broken Hill in a little plane. Everybody was longing to have a drink and I don't mean water! I said, 'Don't worry, Broken Hill is putting on a civic reception for us when we get there and knowing Broken Hill, there'll be some nice beer or scotch or whatever. It'll be right when we get there.' A large crowd met us at the airport and we were taken to the Broken Hill Town Hall where the civic reception was to be held. Would you believe, there were tea, coffee and sandwiches, and not a drop of what we all felt like. After this, I had to go up on the stage with all the local dignitaries, the mayor, the town clerk, chief of police, chief of fire brigade, headmaster of the school, the man who was now

73

secretary and business manager of the hospital which of course was my father's old job, and a few others. All of the opera crowd were lined up in the front row of the Town Hall. All the dignitaries got up and said how excited they were that we should all be in Broken Hill but particularly me. This went on and on, and my gang of people were sitting down there trying not to giggle every now and then. Finally it was just too much, because the mayor was the last to give a speech. He rattled on about us all but particularly about me, saying how proud Broken Hill was of me. He finished by saying, 'June has been a great ambassadress . . . abroad.' Well, pardon me!

Two of the people who travelled with us were a lovely married couple, Robert Gard (Bobby, as we called him) who was one of the Ernestos, and his wife Doreen Morrow, who was my counterpart. Doreen was in the early stages of pregnancy at the time. At the end of the first two weeks of the tour Doreen unfortunately had a miscarriage. Naturally she couldn't do the rest of the tour. This meant that I had to do the rest of the run, another two weeks, singing all the performances. I ended up singing twelve performances in thirteen days and travelling all over the countryside as well. Everybody said they thought I was singing better at the end than I was at the beginning, so I guess I should do these long tours more often!

During the 1970s I was approached by the English Opera Group and asked whether I would like to play the role of Magda in Puccini's *La Rondine*. This was another role that I had heard many times on recording and had often thought I'd very much like to perform. It was quite a different concept from the way it was normally done, in that David Poulteney directed it as if the whole of the second and third acts were a dream. It was only at the end when Magda was discovered in her rocking chair, dressed in the same costume that she was wearing in the first act, and holding the dress that she was going to wear to Chez Bullier, with the mirror ball spinning, as it was in the end of Act I, that the audience realised that the whole thing had been a dream. It was an enchanting concept. When I did the same opera some years later in Australia, we played the normal mini *Traviata*-type production. I missed that dream feeling tremendously.

On Christmas Day 1974 Cyclone Tracy devastated the city of Darwin. A great big concert was arranged in the Sydney Opera House in January 1975 to raise money for the relief fund. I had just arrived in Sydney at the time and I was asked if I would take part in the concert. Of course I was absolutely thrilled to do so. But after that concert lots of lovely things happened to me.

Number one was that for the first time in years I met a dear friend of mine, Dame Joan Hammond, who was at the concert. Dame Joan at that stage was in charge of the Victorian Opera Company. We had a lovely long chat during which she asked me whether I would like to perform for her company. I said I'd be thrilled to do so. At the same concert I was asked if I would care to do some Gildas in *Rigoletto* for the Australian Opera Company. Naturally I jumped at that as well. Both engagements were for that year, 1975. The *Rigoletto*s were a great thrill for me because I hadn't sung Gilda for some time and it is one of my favourite roles.

Way back when I first sang Gilda for Sadler's Wells, I decided that I would die with my eyes open. It was staged in such a way that when I died, my eyes were staring straight out at the audience. When it came to the fact that my father, Rigoletto, realises that he has had his own daughter killed and he says, 'Gilda, Gilda'—Frederick Sharpe, who was playing Rigoletto, spat fair and square in my eye. Of course, I couldn't blink because I was dead! It was burning like hell, and, like all operatic death scenes, it was ages before the curtain came down. So there I was with my eye burning and I couldn't do anything about it. I decided then and there that I would never die again with my eyes open—and I promise you I haven't.

I didn't have a great deal of rehearsal for the Australian production, but luckily I knew the role although, admittedly,

I hadn't sung it in Italian for a long while so I had to re-learn it in Italian. At one of my first rehearsals I was going through my paces when suddenly a gentleman came in. They stopped the rehearsal and introduced me to him as the musical director, Maestro Carlo Felice Cillario. He said that he shouldn't be at the rehearsal but asked us to carry on, which we did. He stayed and after a while took his baton out and started conducting. It was great to work with him, really super! After the rehearsal, he asked me, 'Where did you learn to sing the role like this?' I told him I had studied it originally with my maestro, my singing teacher in London, Dino Borgioli. He said, 'Ah, that explains it!' So there started a lovely relationship between maestro and singer. I was also told afterwards by our accompanist for the day, Caroline Lille, that before he was introduced to me, when he first walked in and I was singing, he turned to her and said, 'At last we have a Gilda.'

My father, Rigoletto, was a terrific Australian baritone called Raymond Myers. Gilda was in a sack and he had to pull the sack down to the river bank, not knowing it was his daughter inside. At one particular performance Ray couldn't get the sack open so he was singing 'Gilda, Gilda,' etc., and he couldn't even see me. I was singing with my head in the sack! It really was quite hysterical. When the press notices came out they said, 'Mr Myers must have been psychic to realise it was his daughter in the sack.' The banks of the river were made of foam rubber and, at another performance, when Ray was being very dramatic, realising he had sent his own daughter to her death, he stood on the foam rubber and ended up falling into the river, much to everybody's delight, except his own. What a great performer he is, and what a great voice!

That season I only did five performances but they went very well indeed, and I was very thrilled to have been asked to work with the Australian Opera Company.

Then it was down to Melbourne for the Victorian Opera Company. The two operas they had offered me were

Donizetti's *Maria Stuarda (Mary Stuart)*, which we did in English with me in the title role, and *Don Pasquale*, in which I sang Norina. It was marvellous to do the *Mary Stuart* because not long before I came back to Australia in 1974, I had seen Janet Baker perform the role for the English National Opera. It was very exciting and Baker had been tremendous, as usual. What a glorious voice and what a beautiful performer!

We were going to do the version for two sopranos, with another soprano singing the role of Queen Elizabeth I, which is arguably the way it was written. Our Queen Elizabeth was a fantastic Australian soprano, Nance Grant. The whole production was beautifully staged and designed and directed by Robin Lovejoy, literally on a shoe-string, with great finesse and artistry. The scenery was really quite brilliant. The costuming was elegant but not expensive. It all proved that a production can still be beautifully mounted on a smallish budget. I was very honoured to be part of that successful production and I loved singing that exciting role of Mary Stuart.

The *Don Pasquale* was quite different from any production I'd ever done of that opera. It was directed by a wonderful English director, Dennis Arundell. I had worked with him before at Sadler's Wells. He is a marvellous director and a terrific disciplinarian and did he ever know his Donizetti! He said that we were to forget any productions of this opera that we had done before, that we were getting back to Donizetti's original concept, particularly as far as the recitatives were concerned. This was my fourth production of *Don Pasquale*, but when Dennis Arundell started explaining things to us I thought how exciting it was to be approaching the opera from a completely different angle. For instance, Norina is a poor widow, yet in every production I've ever done, in her first scene she was in a charming boudoir in her house, elegantly furnished. She was beautifully gowned. It suddenly registered with me that it didn't ring true. Arundell explained to me what he thought her bedroom would be like and what her maid would look like – not a pretty smart little maid but quite a sleazy one. I should not be in a pretty gown but in an ordinary wraparound dressing-gown affair, with my hair in a turban and nothing on my feet. He said, 'I want you picking your toes.' Of course I shrieked with laughter and he said, 'That's the sort of thing that Norina would probably do.' So I went into the whole thing very lightheartedly and, in a way, very excitedly. It turned out to be a delightful, witty and clever production and I was thrilled to be part of it.

As a result of the success of the *Rigoletto* that year, the Australian Opera asked me to come back the following year, 1976, to do it again, as well as Rosina in Rossini's *The Barber of Seville*; Blonde in Mozart's *Il Seraglio* and two Gilbert and Sullivans, Josephine in *HMS Pinafore* and Phyllis in *Iolanthe*. I got back from England in May 1976 and the first opera I rehearsed was *The Barber of Seville*. This was the first time I'd ever played the role or sung it, and I had been very busy learning it in London so when I arrived I knew it perfectly, which was just as well, because I only had three days rehearsal before I did the production! We performed at the Adelaide Festival Theatre, where the company was doing a season. So I was thrown in at the deep end. However, I did manage to have one quick dress rehearsal on the stage at the Festival Theatre. It was the first time I'd seen the set or the production and it was quite delightful. It was mostly black and white, with just the occasional splash of colour, and it really was charming. The central part of the set was like a two-storey pagoda with lots of doors for all the entrances and exits. After a while, I was totally confused. I came out of one of the doors and said, 'What do I do now?' Donald Shanks, who was playing one of the bass roles, said, 'This is where you sing "Vilja".' To which I replied, 'I wish to God it was!'

Then it was back to Sydney to sing Gilda in *Rigoletto* again. This was an even greater success than it had been the year before. During one performance, while I was singing

'Tutte le Feste al tempio' I suddenly realised that Cillario had put his baton down and was leaning back against the orchestra rail. I thought that it was very strange. Towards the end of the aria, when it gets very animated, he picked up the baton and started conducting again. After the performance, I asked him, 'Maestro, why did you put your baton down and not conduct for some of the "Tutte le Feste"?'

He replied, 'You were singing it so beautifully, June, the orchestra were listening to you and accompanying you beautifully, so I thought I'll put my baton down and I'll sit back and I'll enjoy it!'

I thought that was wonderful.

Another lovely thing happened during that season. The *Australian* newspaper every year used to name what its critics thought where the best moments in theatre, television, opera, ballet and so on. The best operatic moment they chose for 1976 was the Vendetta duet between Rigoletto and Gilda, with Raymond Myers and June Bronhill!

Il Seraglio was a delightful production. It was particularly thrilling for me because I was going to work with the Australian soprano, Joan Carden, for the first time since the beginning of the 1960s, when Joan had worked with me in *The Merry Widow*. We hadn't seen each other for all those years but it was just like a wonderful old friendship starting up all over again. She's a divine singer and a lovely performer and we had lots and lots of good laughs together. It was actually during *Il Seraglio* that Carden came up with a phrase that I quite often quote. One day we were sitting in the Green Room at the Opera House in Sydney when she suddenly said to me, out of the blue, 'Get off the table, Mabel, the two quid's for the beer.' That phrase has stuck ever since and I just love it. Mabel is a pet name which lots of my dear friends call me.

Il Seraglio was rather fun for me, too, because Osmin was played by Donald Shanks, a wonderful Australian bass who has had great success singing all over the world. Don is about six feet four inches and I am four feet eleven inches. In the wonderful duet where Blonde is laying down the law to Osmin, Don absolutely towered over me. It looked unbelievably funny. The audience just fell about laughing and adored it.

Then there were the two Gilbert and Sullivan operas. They were super for me because, apart from the fun of performing, they introduced me to two people who have remained dear friends ever since. The man playing the comic roles of Sir Joseph Porter and the Lord Chancellor is a wonderful singer, actor, performer and pianist, Dennis Olsen. The other one was one of our directors, a delightful love called Brian Crossley. It really was all tremendous fun and I suddenly saw Gilbert and Sullivan in quite a different light, because the productions were not done in the traditional manner, the D'Oyly Carte copyright having expired some years before. I discovered that all of Gilbert and Sullivan's heroines are really rather dizzy blondes and if you play them in that slightly dizzy way, very deadpan, dizzy blonde fashion, that's how you get the laughs. I learnt a lot from that season.

One thing that I find quite extraordinary is that although that Australian Opera season of mine was a tremendous success — over seventy performances in six months — I've never been asked to work for the company again!

It's quite amazing, really, that in all of my professional career I had never done any Gilbert and Sullivan until this moment and then it suddenly snowballed. As a result of the two I'd done for the Australian Opera, the Western Australia Opera Company asked me to play Yum Yum in *The Mikado* and Gianetta in *The Gondoliers*. Around this time also I did *Pinafore* in Melbourne, Canberra and Adelaide for various companies — all of this, I might tell you, at the ripe old age of forty-seven! Then over the last few years I've been working for a young company in Melbourne, called the Melbourne Music Theatre, in which I've gone the other way. I've seen performing roles like Katisha in *The Mikado*, the Duchess of Plazatoro in *The Gondoliers* and recently I did the Queen of the Fairies in *Iolanthe* – all mezzo soprano roles!

The Mikado in Western Australia was tremendous fun. We did it in the enormous Perth Entertainment Centre, which seats about 8,000 people, but it can be blocked off to seat less. We were playing on an average to about 3,500 to 4,000 people a night, sometimes even more. I also did this production not long after I'd had an operation to remove my wretched bunions, which had really given me a lot of pain, and I had to wear special little sandal-type shoes which were quite appropriate for the role. I couldn't walk properly. I was still re-learning to walk which was also good because all I could do was shuffle along, so I was able to portray the Japanese way of walking almost to perfection. It was an excellent production – enormous, as you can imagine, on this vast stage, but it worked remarkably well.

At one particular performance, at the beginning of Act II when Yum Yum was being prepared by her sisters and friends for her wedding to Nanki-Poo, and the girls were singing the lovely chorus, 'Braid the Raven Hair', I was sitting there, making-up my face and so on, when suddenly the girls all looked at me with very funny old-fashioned looks on their faces. I wondered what they were all sniggering about. I turned around and there was Brian Crossley, our director, in the most outrageous kimono you've ever seen in your life, with an extraordinary big Japanese wig with knitting needles and balls of wools going through it. His tiny gold-rimmed glasses were on the end of his nose and he was carrying a leather attaché case. All the girls were still singing and I was acknowledging everything. Brian looked up at me and said, 'Avon calling' in a Japanese accent. I didn't bat an eyelid, I just took it all in. When I came offstage, though, I said to Brian, 'That was absolutely wonderful – where did you get it?'

'Never mind all of that, you didn't even laugh.'

'You try to send me up on stage and you've had it – I can send up people on stage but it's very difficult to send *me* up on stage. I was laughing inwardly, but I wouldn't do it outwardly, Brian – you would have been ashamed of me, wouldn't you?'

He said, 'I guess I would.'

At another performance, however, quite an extraordinary thing happened. The curtain had gone up on Act II and the girls were again singing 'Braid the Raven Hair' and preparing me for my wedding, when suddenly I was aware of a rumbling noise. The stage felt as if it were shaking and I thought, 'Dear God, it's an earthquake.' Then I was aware of things falling, coming from above us and around us, like little bits of metal, and I thought, 'If this is somebody's idea of a joke, it's a very poor one.' Then from the flies an incredible pole fell down and landed on the stage, brushing one of the girls, who was quite dazed by it. It could have been a tragedy. The orchestra was still playing while all this stuff was rattling around us and there were great big elastic bands and metal hooks all over the stage. I told the orchestra to stop and told the girls not to move. Then the staff naturally came on to the stage to see what it was. It turned out that it was a screen for films and slide-shows, which was very rarely used, and which was kept together up there in the flies by hooks and these big elastic bands. It hadn't been used for so long that the elastic bands had perished and the pole had fallen down from the bottom of the screen. I called for the St John's Ambulance people to come up on stage to attend to the girl who had been hit. Everybody on stage was stunned; the whole audience was stunned. Then the St John's Ambulance woman tripped and fell as she came on to the stage, so we had to get *two* St John's Ambulance fellows! They then pulled down the curtain and the safety curtain, and started to check everything up in the flies. I said, 'I'm not going back on there until I know for a fact that everything has been thoroughly checked, and I'm sure I speak for the company as well.'

When the curtain had been down for about ten minutes, I said to the stage manager, 'Do you think I ought to go out and chat to the audience and tell them exactly what's happened – perhaps tell them a couple of jokes?'

'Would you do that, June?'

'Of course.' So I went out and told them what had happened, and told them a couple of jokes. Then I said, 'Well as I'm in this Japanese costume, I'm not going to let the moment pass! I'll sing "One Fine Day" from *Madame Butterfly* in costume, as I'm sure I'll never have the opportunity of doing so again.' So, unaccompanied, I sang 'One Fine Day' and then about four or five other things.

I looked into the wings and saw Tom Edmonds, who was singing Nanki-Poo. I called him on stage and said, 'Come on, love, we'll do a couple of duets together.' So we sang a couple of unaccompanied duets and then I told him that he had to sing an aria, and he decided he would sing 'M'Appari' from the opera *Martha*. Unfortunately he started it a bit too high. He stopped in midstream and said, 'I'll never get the top notes,' so I said, 'Well, you carry on and I'll have a go at the top notes!' Well, of course, the audience were in fits of laughter by this time. Tom and I entertained them for three quarters of an hour while everything was being checked in the flies and on stage. When it was all ready I quickly went to my dressing-room for a couple of minutes and powdered my face, and we started from the beginning of Act II again, as if nothing had happened.

The Western Australian Opera Company, apart from asking me to do Gianetta in *The Gondoliers*, also asked me to do Blonde in their new production of *Il Seraglio* which was opening their new home, the old His Majesty's Theatre. They had completely refurbished the place and it was quite magnificent. They had also bought the old His Majesty's Hotel next door, and the bars of the hotel were incorporated into the theatre. One bar in particular absolutely amazed me when I saw the new place for the first time because it was a full-length bar, not like an ordinary little theatre bar, and it was wonderful marble. They had maintained the facade and the wonderful staircase. They had dressing-room space for 140-odd people, not counting band rooms for the orchestra. It was all quite incredible.

In this production of *Il Seraglio* I had the joy of working with the marvellous bass, Noel Mangin, who played Osmin. We had a lot of fun together. The Constanza was a terrific Australian soprano, Margaret Haggart. Maggie was great fun. She was similar in size to me, both of us a couple of short plumpies! Maggie always used to wear platform-soled shoes, with about an inch-high platform and four-inch heels. One day I asked, 'Maggie, why do you wear those shoes?'

'I've got to look taller, June.'

'You can't wear them on stage.'

'Oh, yes, I can! I've worn these in every production I've ever done—even in *Traviata*.'

Of course I fell about laughing, because I don't care what anyone says, you can't walk elegantly in shoes like that!

The other opera company that I've worked with here in Australia is the South Australian Opera Company. They asked me to do Magda in *La Rondine* and the role of Rosalinda in their new production of *Die Fledermaus*. I was rather chuffed that they asked me to sing the role of Rosalinda, having always sung Adele in the past. By then I think I was getting a bit long in the tooth for playing the juvenile roles like Adele. Anyway, I was thrilled to play Rosalinda and we had a marvellous soprano, Carolyn Vaughan, playing Adele.

Carolyn is tall and slim and I am short and plump. In the ballroom scene in Act II, when Rosalinda sees her maid, Adele, flaunting herself in one of her gowns and comments, 'There's my maid—*and* in one of my gowns,' I did the biggest double-take imaginable, wondering how one of my gowns could possibly fit her. The audience got the joke and it got a marvellous laugh.

Although these days I don't think of myself as an opera singer, it's amazing how many people still classify me as one. In fact my career has diversified over the years. While I haven't sung much opera in recent years, I still love singing opera and always include a lot of operatic arias in my concerts. I must admit that I'm still open to suggestions and offers for operas but not if they are roles that don't suit me. For instance, recently I was actually offered the title role in Puccini's opera, *Turandot*. They had to be joking!

8

The Sound of Music

When I agreed to play the role of Maria in Garnet Carroll's 1961 Australian production of *The Sound of Music*, I signed a run-of-the-play contract, really thinking that it would run six to eight months at the most. The money that I was offered – the Australian equivalent of $US1,000 a week – was really pretty good money then. I thought I would save up quite a considerable amount of it and go to Italy to study with Toti dal Monte because while I was in Australia doing *The Merry Widow* Dino Borgioli had died and I was left without a singing teacher. I had always admired Toti dal Monte so I thought I'd hunt her out in Italy, just as I had hunted Dino out in London, and if she accepted me I would study with her and really get back into a full-time operatic career. Well, of course, *The Sound of Music* ran and ran, so that was the end of those plans!

Another thing that inspired me to play the role of Maria was the fact that Charles Hickman, my wonderful friend and the director of other shows I had done for Sadler's Wells, was going to direct it. At the time we met in London and discussed the whole production, the London production, starring Jean Bayliss, was on at the Palace Theatre. We saw it and absolutely adored it, although honestly, we both thought that it was just a bit slow. But it was inspiring and gave me a lot of encouragement. Also in that cast was Constance Shacklock who had hailed from the Royal Opera House, Covent Garden, to play the Mother Abbess. I had met Constance a few times, so I decided I'd go backstage and say hello to her and make myself known to Jean Bayliss. It was lovely meeting Jean because she was absolutely enchanting and thrilled about my doing the show in

Australia. We discussed all sorts of pitfalls in the role of Maria. Then I went to see Constance. When I knocked on her door, she didn't say 'Come in', she said, 'Ave', same as the Mother Abbess does in the show! She was still in her costume and her dressing-table was on a slightly raised platform, almost as if it were an altar, and the room had icons, statues, candles and on the dressing-table – it looked like a Mother Abbess' room. Of course, I contained myself – I didn't giggle, as I'm prone to do in such situations.

We eventually flew to Australia in August 1961 and started our rehearsal period. The sets were absolutely wonderful and no expense was spared, as I have found in so many Australian productions – if they're going to do a thing in Australia, they really do it well. Garnet Carroll had assembled all the right people for this one and it really was an excellent cast. I had learnt to strum a few chords on the guitar in London so that I could cope with having to play it in 'Do Re Mi' and 'Edelweiss'. I've got very little hands, so I had great difficulty putting my fingers into the right position. I had lots of publicity photos taken with the children, with me supposedly playing the guitar quite professionally.

I had the most beautiful set of children imaginable and of course, because of the laws about the number of shows young children can perform in a week, it meant that we had to have three sets of the very young ones. But it was worth it, because they were quite wonderful! Our Baron von Trapp was a wonderful English actor called Peter Graves – tall, elegant, aristocratic and with the most wicked sense of humour I've ever come across. You never knew what he was going to say or do next. He used to say a few things in front of the children that slightly embarrassed me – I even found myself blushing a couple of times! He used some pretty strong language but I'm sure the children really didn't know what the words meant – at least I hope not!

Our Mother Abbess was Rosina Raisbeck, a fellow Australian whom I had met in London. She was working with Covent Garden Opera and I thought she would be absolutely ideal for the role. I got in touch with Garnet Carroll in Australia and said, 'I don't know whether you've cast anybody as the Mother Abbess as yet but I don't think you can go beyond Rosina Raisbeck and I'm sure that if she's available she'd just jump at it. You couldn't wish for anybody better.' Mr Carroll got in touch with Rosie and she was thrilled to do the role. She was quite fantastic—tall, beautiful, a wonderful actress with a marvellous voice and the best Mother Abbess ever, in my opinion.

Our Elsa Schraeder was a delicious actress called Lola Brooks—not the greatest of voices but a really lovely performer. Max Detweiler was a terrific character man, Eric Reiman. We had a delightful girl playing Liesl, Julie Day— she sang very prettily, looked divine and danced like a dream. Rolf was a young man called Tony Jenkins—what a voice that young man had! He really was quite lovely. His duet with Julie was beautifully staged and performed.

We were all very excited about the opening night and eventually, on 20 September 1961, it arrived. I have never experienced the same excitement—apart from *The Merry Widow*—as was generated throughout the theatre and into our dressing-rooms over the Tannoy that night. When the children made their appearance on stage, the audience just went absolutely berserk. There is an old saying—you should never appear on a stage with children or animals! I turned to Peter Graves, who was standing next to me, and out of the corner of my mouth said, 'All we need is for a dog to come on behind them and we'll be really home and hosed.'

It was great, a tremendous success, and I was very happy to be part of that production. I was lucky to have such beautiful children—they really were delightful and not in the least precocious. They all called me Mummy; I almost became their second mum! When we were all offstage at the same time, they would all flock into my dressing-room and sit around talking to me and asking me questions. They were too good for words.

Autographing a programme for a fan at the stage-door
after *Lucia di Lammermoor*.

A great welcome from George and Daisy and other fans at Broken Hill airport in 1960, when June made her first visit to Australia since leaving for England in 1952.

The two *Adeles* from *Die Fledermaus* (1959), Marion Studholme (*left*) and June Bronhill.

June Bronhill and John Larsen in the 1960 Australian production of *The Merry Widow*.

The Sadler's Wells production of *La Vie Parisienne* in 1960: a scene from the show and June in her dressing-room.

Unfortunately, during the run of *The Sound of Music* I became quite ill and had to have an operation. I was off the show for four weeks. My understudy, a charming English singer and actress called Vanessa Lee, took over. I had met her a few times in London and she was also married to Peter Graves. When I was better, but still not well enough to go on stage, I went to see the show and it seemed strange to be sitting up there in the circle watching somebody else playing my role!

At matinees, there were generally a couple of hundred schoolchildren attending, naturally with teachers in charge. After the performance they would all be lined up at the stage-door to get a glimpse of us as we left the theatre. It was rather hard work at the stage-door, so I got the doorman to bring them into my dressing-room in groups of eight at a time and I would sign their autograph books and have a little chat with them. Consequently, on matinee days I rarely had time to have a proper break! But it was worth it. They were our audience of the future. It's amazing the number of people in their thirties today who have said to me that they saw me in *The Sound of Music* when they were at school. I love it!

One of the best audiences we had was actually at a preview. It was a theatre full of nuns and they were hilarious. They laughed at things which we thought were very serious and which no one laughed at in any other performance. One of the best laughs from the nuns was when I knelt at the feet of the Mother Abbess and said, 'Mother, I am ready to take the vows of poverty, obedience and chastity' – and they shrieked!

Rosina as the Mother Abbess was all that I had predicted. She was quite splendid. She used to have all the nuns in fear and trepidation before every performance because she would line them up and check them for watches, rings, bracelets and, of course, nail polish. If anybody had any of these things on, boom, they were charged quickly back to the dressing-room to get rid of them. She really was a martinet but wonderful – everybody loved her. But one night

Rosie was a bit late arriving at the theatre because she'd had to go to a special cocktail party. When it came to my first scene with her, I knocked on the door and she said, 'Ave.' I walked in and said, 'You wanted to see me, Mother Abbess.' She came towards me and said, 'Yes, Maria.' She held out her hand for me to kiss and there, shining up at me, were the longest and reddest nails you've ever seen in your life! So out of the upstage corner of my mouth I said, 'Nails.' She looked at me, then looked down at her hand and almost froze on the spot. She did the rest of the scene with her fists clenched so that nobody could possibly see her red fingernails.

The theatre had a great big photo display of me but without my name, just lovely photographs and record covers in a great big window. Just before a matinee, a friend who was coming in for the show overheard two dear old things talking and looking at the display. One said, 'You know, I've seen every one of her films – that June Allyson.'

It's absolutely marvellous being associated with a long and successful run, but one of the drawbacks, unfortunately, is that sometimes we tend to go on what we call 'automatic pilot'. I remember at one Saturday matinee I sang my opening number, 'The Sound of Music', and suddenly I found myself walking off the stage as I always did, singing the last three words of the song and I couldn't remember singing any of it! I remembered the curtain going up, me sitting up there in the tree eating my apple and throwing the core away, and then getting down from the tree, but the rest of it was nothing to do with *The Sound of Music* at all. I had completely planned my Sunday dinner, how I was going to seat everyone at the table, what wine I was going to serve, everything. That brought me up with one hell of a jolt! So after that, I had to start re-thinking every line I said so that I could get a new perspective, try to feel that I had never heard the line before. People say, 'How can you do it?' but it's amazing how you can do it. You really have to try to approach everything from a completely new angle;

otherwise you get into an awful rut. I'm happy to say it worked. Nothing else like that happened for the rest of the run, which was eleven months in Melbourne. Then we transferred to Sydney.

In Sydney new children had to be auditioned because the Melbourne children couldn't travel with us. We had Julie Day, who played Liesl, of course. I had to be at the auditions. They were really quite lovely at the audition but when it came to performing they were the absolute opposites of my sweet little Melbourne boys and girls. They had mostly come from theatre schools and had those pushy theatre mums – thank God I didn't have one! They were lovely but cheeky little devils. One of them, though, Sharon McKittrick, grew up to become quite a dear friend of mine.

Recently when I was doing *The Pirates of Penzance* (which you'll read about later on) in Sydney, the stage doorman said that somebody called Maxine wanted to see me and had said that I knew her. I said, 'I don't know any Maxine that I can think of, but it doesn't matter, send her in.' A tall, blonde, elegant young woman came in and said in a rather deepish voice, 'Don't you recognise me, June?'

'I'm terribly sorry, Maxine, but I must be honest – I don't.'

'I was Frederick in your Sydney cast of *The Sound of Music.*'

Of course, that was too much for me. I nearly died. Then Maxine explained that she was now with that wonderful show in Sydney which had been running for umpteen years called *Les Girls*! And that was my Frederick!

The Sound of Music was going swimmingly in Sydney, and because it was such a success, the management decided to put out a souvenir programme. During the interval at one performance, someone asked me if I'd seen the souvenir programme. I said I didn't know it was out.

'Well, it's worth reading.'

So I got a copy. To my horror, it said that I had learned to play the guitar especially for *The Sound of Music* and that now I could be considered a virtuoso of the instrument! That made me shriek with laughter because I could only still play about six chords. I couldn't even tune the thing, I had to get the guitar player from the orchestra to come to my dressing-room every night and do it for me. At the end of that performance I made a marvellous curtain speech about the programme. Apart from things about me, lots of things about the cast were completely wrong, so I had a great time sending up our souvenir programme. I don't think Johnny Carroll appreciated it very much and I apologised to him. John didn't know it was out – he hadn't even proofread it!

And another thing that happened during *The Sound of Music* in Sydney was that I became pregnant! But I'll talk about that later. Naturally I couldn't stay with the show for the rest of its run and I left when I was about five months pregnant. I was still bouncing up and down on the bed singing 'The Lonely Goatherd' when I left. Nobody had a clue about me being pregnant because it didn't show – they had to let my costumes out about an inch at the waist, but that was all. That was the end of me and *The Sound of Music*, until it came back into my life many years later.

After I'd had my darling daughter, Garnet Carroll asked me if I would do a revival of *The Merry Widow* in 1963. I was thrilled and I jumped at it. It was going to be performed in a couple of cities, Newcastle and Brisbane, where I'd never performed it before.

An extraordinary thing happened at one performance in Newcastle. My usual practice was that, as I finished singing 'Vilja' with my arms up in the air, if the audience was still applauding after I had very slowly taken them down to my sides, then I would walk forward and do the pinspot encore. I had finished singing the song and I was walking down to the front for the encore. Suddenly I saw a man coming down the centre aisle towards me. I was a little bit anxious and hoped he wasn't going to do something awful, like throw something at me! But he just stopped behind the orchestra rail and said, 'Will you sing it again, just for me?'

I said, 'Of course I will,' so I sang it again, directly to him and just for him. He was bowled over. The audience went wild, so I had to sing it again, just for them!

During the next few years I was involved in lots of exciting shows, both in England and in Australia, but I want to talk about them in the next couple of chapters and finish this chapter with more about some of my favourite musicals.

In May 1978 the Queensland Lyric Opera Company asked me if I would like to play the role of Teresa in *The Maid of the Mountains*. I was excited because I'd sung a lovely song from *The Maid of the Mountains*, 'Love will Find a Way', many times in concerts, clubs and cabarets. It was being directed and choreographed by a very dear friend and a brilliant lady of Australian theatre, Betty Pounder. She was wonderful to work with and we had marvellous times.

It was a lovely production, except for one little mishap. It was about our first dress rehearsal and the sets were almost finished. My role, Teresa, is a gypsy girl and I had to wear a marvellous gypsy costume with high-heeled boots. As she was leaving all the brigands, Teresa sang a lovely farewell to them. Pounder said to me, 'Miss June, do you think you could actually be climbing up through the mountains while you're singing the farewell?' I said, 'Well, I'll give it a go, Pounder.' Cut into the 'mountains' were some steps which hadn't been finished. Neither had the set at the top of the mountains, where Teresa ended up singing. I started up the steps and I thought, 'My word, these steps are steep!' Then I realised that they'd been put in back to front—the riser should have been the tread. So we had a short tread and a high riser. With my short legs and the high-heeled boots it was very difficult. Near the top I felt myself teetering. I thought, 'Oh dear, I'm going to fall.' I pulled myself together but I started teetering again and there was nothing to hold on to. I stopped singing in mid-stream and tried to balance myself but I couldn't, and down I toppled. I rolled down about two or three steps but the rest I fell, bang-slap, on to the stage. I just missed hitting my head on a counterweight. Everybody was in a dreadful state and I was, too, of course! The most incredible thing about this fall was that it felt like slow motion, and when I told the boys of this feeling they said that watching me they had felt the same – they had wanted to rush to me, but couldn't move. Luckily, all I got out of the fall was a badly bruised bottom and a small graze in the same area. The worst thing about it was that I now have a horror of staircases, whereas before I'd never worried about staircases at all. Now they worry me, not only on stage but off stage as well. For all that, I loved doing *The Maid of the Mountains* and working with that wonderful Betty Pounder.

The next thing on the agenda, musical-comedy-wise, was that wonderful musical by Stephen Sondheim, *A Little Night Music*. The director, Rob Hatherley asked me to play the role of Desirée Armfeldt. I was very excited and jumped at it, because, a few years before in England when I was doing a summer season in Great Yarmouth, I had word that Hal Prince would like to hear me sing and read for the Broadway production but the only place he could meet me would be in Paris. I could only get to Paris from Great Yarmouth and back in time for my first show at 6.30 if I chartered a plane. So I did! I met Hal Prince in Paris and sang for him. Then I read some of the lines. He seemed to be quite impressed and he said he would arrange for me to sing for Sondheim in London. Then he asked me, 'Are you staying overnight?'

'Oh, no, I have to get back – I have two performances tonight.'

'Good heavens, where?'

'Great Yarmouth. It's in Norfolk in East Anglia.'

'How did you get here?'

'I chartered a plane.'

He was nonplussed – he couldn't believe anybody would charter a plane for an audition.

The sad thing was that I didn't get the part – wonderful Glynis Johns got it. I believe she was great. I wish I'd seen her.

So I jumped at the chance of doing this production in Sydney with Rob Hatherley. It turned out to be super. We had a wonderful young orchestra, the Western Sinfonia, conducted by their musical director, Bransby Byrne. The orchestra was situated behind the actors and concealed amongst the trees of the garden. This meant that the conductor was standing behind us, which is not the easiest way to conduct any performance, least of all a Sondheim score. But it worked wonderfully. It had a tremendous success and a lot of people said to us afterwards that they thought our production was better than the original Sydney production some years earlier.

The woman who played the role of my mother was a wonderful English comedienne–singer–actress–musician– you name it, she does it–Colleen Clifford. She had been living in Australia for many years, and she was really quite delightful. We have maintained a beautiful friendship for years and we will for as long as we're both around. This is the lovely thing about working with people for the first time–you make so many new friends. Another friend I made during that production was our musical director, Bransby Byrne. Since then he has been my official accompanist on nearly every concert tour I've done. We have a terrific rapport. He knows exactly what I'm going to do next–he reads me like a book. He is a wonderful musician and a great accompanist.

In January 1981 I had a phone call from Ross Taylor of Ross Taylor Productions in London. He said they were going to do a revival of *The Sound of Music* and he would very much like me to play the role of the Mother Abbess.

I said, 'Ross, it's not written for my sort of voice; it's written for a mezzo soprano, a much deeper voice than mine, and I just couldn't sing it as it's written.'

'We'll do anything you want. We're more than happy to accommodate you in any way.'

'Well, if I do sing it, certainly "Climb Every Mountain" would have to be transposed up a third.'

'June, it doesn't worry us. We'll do whatever you want, because we definitely want you to come over and do the role of the Mother Abbess.'

I asked him who else was in the cast.

'It looks pretty certain that we've got Petula Clark to play Maria.'

'Ooh!' I said.

'Yes, a lot of people are saying "Ooh",' he said. 'Honor Blackman – remember her from "The Avengers"? – is playing Elsa Schraeder.'

'Terrific.'

'A marvellous actor called Michael Jayston who's worked with the Royal Shakespeare Company is playing von Trapp and a terrific actor called John Bennett is playing Max Detweiler.'

It all sounded very exciting so I said he could count me in. It seemed a super company to work with, and it was exciting to be going back to London for such a terrific project. We had a marvellous American director called John Fearnley who was lovely. He had had a lot to do with the various productions of *The Sound of Music* in America. Pet Clark was amazing. She looked twenty and was so petite, with a gamin haircut. Honor was tremendous, quite unlike anybody else I've ever seen in the role of Elsa. She was not bitchy in the role; she was lovely, elegant, totally believable. Michael Jayston was great as Baron von Trapp, and John Bennett couldn't have been bettered as Max Detweiler.

The sets were out of this world. I'm sure many people will remember the terrace scene from the movie, where Elsa, realising that the Baron is in love with Maria, bows graciously out of his life. The way Honor did it was very moving. The set we had for that scene had lovely garden furniture and at the back was a hedge with wrought-iron gates, on which were semi-rampant horses – a replica of the von Trapp estate outside Salzburg. Beyond that was just a backcloth but it looked like a lake surrounded by mountains because the lighting achieved an incredible impression of depth. As Elsa made her exit the sun began to set behind the mountains. It was the most lifelike sunset I've ever seen in theatre. It gave such meaning to her final words as she said to the Baron, 'One thing they don't have in Vienna, Georg, that you have here – the sunsets. I shall miss them.' The scene concluded with the sun disappearing behind the mountains; not just in colour, you saw the sun actually disappear. The sky changed to that wonderful colour of evening and gradually darkened to a velvety blue and as that happened, the stars began to twinkle and the villages around the lake began to glow as their lights appeared. It looked as if it went for miles, and was completely and utterly breathtaking. At every performance it got a round of applause – deservedly.

My 'Climb Every Mountain' stopped the show at every performance and I had to do an encore, which was exciting for me. Before we opened the show was sold out for about three months in advance. After about ten months of capacity business, London was hit by the Falklands Islands crisis and naturally everyone wanted to stay home and listen to the radio or watch TV for the next news bulletin. Business in all the theatres dropped off. At times we were playing to about half houses, perhaps a little bit more, and we were all a little anxious. Then one night we thought about it and realised that the theatre we were playing in seated 2,500 people, so we were probably playing to about 1,300 people, which is larger than the capacity of an average theatre. So it wasn't bad really.

The Sound of Music was a production that I will remember for ever. We ran for fifteen months. Ross Raylor put a marvellous message in all our dressing-rooms before opening night, a quote from Oscar Hammerstein: 'A revival of any show has to be twice as good as the original, because everybody remembers the original to be twice as good as it was.' Very true!

On one of my nights off during the show I took my daughter – who was visiting me from New Zealand – to see

the new Broadway version of *The Pirates of Penzance*. I don't
know when I've laughed so much in my life, or enjoyed
anything so much. I said to my daughter, 'Do you know,
darling, I'd love to have played the role of Ruth. It's such
fun – it's terrific.' Little did I realise that two years later I
would be playing Ruth in the Australian production of the
Broadway production of *The Pirates of Penzance*!

When I got back to Australia I discovered that an
Australian revival of *The Sound of Music* was underway. They
were about to cast and go into rehearsal, and I thought it
would be lovely to be in it and play the Mother Abbess. As
things turned out, they didn't want me. They wanted a mezzo
soprano. I was a little disconsolate but it was a case of one
door shutting and another door opening. I had a marvellous
phone call from Noel Ferrier. He asked me if I would be
interested in playing Ruth in the Australian production of
The Pirates of Penzance. I flipped. I couldn't believe it!

'I had no idea we were going to do it out here,' I said.

'Yes, we are, and we want you in it.'

'Terrific! I'm all for it. Who else is in it?'

Noel told me that they had Jon English playing the
Pirate King. He is a wonderful rock singer and he had taken
Australian by storm when he played Judas in the Australian
production of *Jesus Christ Superstar*. He was quite incredible
and I think probably the best Judas the show ever had. Simon
Gallagher, a lovely, light pop ballad singer, was playing
Frederick and they had discovered a sweet girl in busking
Melbourne called Marina Prior and decided that she was
the ideal Mable. She had never set foot on a stage in her
life. A marvellous dancer called David Atkins was going to
be the Sergeant of Police and John Wood, whom I had
worked with in opera, was playing the Major General. It
was a top-line cast. The Australian Elizabethan Theatre
Trust was co-producers with the Victoria State Opera. One
of the resident conductors of the Victoria State Opera was
Andrew Green, a bundle of energy, and he was our musical
director. From America came two men who had been

associated with the American *Pirates*, John Ferraro, the director, and Craig Schaefer, the choreographer. The production was a replica—costumes, sets, the lot—of the original American production devised by Joseph Papp. The company was a very happy one. The girls, the pirates, the policemen were all a delight and so very funny. I don't know when I've had such fun with a show.

Jon English is perhaps the greatest professional I've ever worked with and that's saying something. He was brilliantly funny. We called his voice a sort of gravel pit voice but it worked well. He used to do funny things sometimes, like suddenly swinging into the full operatic baritone sound. He had us all eating out of his hands.

We didn't do *Pirates* in one long season; we did three years of short seasons. In the first year, 1984, we opened in Melbourne for six weeks, then twelve weeks in Sydney, then three weeks in Adelaide, and then three weeks in Perth, which was about a twenty-four-week tour. The following year, 1985, we did a return five-week season in Sydney, then went up to Brisbane for eight weeks. That was a thirteen-week season. In 1986 we did another five weeks in Melbourne, then up to Brisbane for another six weeks. Everywhere we went, we played to capacity houses. I think we still have to do return seasons to Adelaide and Perth. In Adelaide we only did three weeks in the wonderful Adelaide Festival Theatre and it was packed to overflowing. We averaged four complete standing ovations a week. Fantastic!

When we were doing our second season in Brisbane, one day Simon Gallagher (who, by the way, sang like a dream as Frederick) and one of the girls from the show got a taxi to the theatre. Simon said he wanted to go to the Queensland Performing Arts Centre.

'Oh, that's where, um, *Pirates of Penzance* is on, isn't it?' said the driver.

'Yes.'

'Oh, they've got that lovely little singer in it—Joan Bromfield.'

Simon seemed to think that the driver should have recognised *him*! (He lives in Queensland and is well known all over Australia.)

Once again, I made lots of lovely new friends working in *Pirates*. For instance, Marina Prior, who has done many wonderful things in between our various productions of *Pirates*, is a dear friend of mine. If she has any problems or is anxious about a role she's doing, she's on the phone to me straight away. Simon Gallagher and I see other quite often and chat on the phone. I'm sorry to say I haven't seen Jon English since doing the show but I'd love to very much; I feel we are great mates. All sorts of other friends were made during that production. That's what show business is all about.

9

Robert and Elizabeth

While I was in Newcastle in January 1964 playing in *The Merry Widow*, I had a cable from Wendy Toye. She asked if I would be interested in playing the role of Elizabeth Arrett (that's what the cable actually said) in a musical based on the Barretts of Wimpole Street. I immediately realised that they meant Elizabeth Barrett, the poet, and I thought, 'What a wonderfully exciting idea!' I immediately phoned Wendy in London and said I was very interested. She told me that Robert Browning was going to be played by Keith Michell, our wonderful Australian actor, who is also a brilliant musician, has a wonderful voice and is a marvellous painter. A well-known actor, John Clements, was playing Edward Moulton Barrett, Elizabeth's father; the music was being written by another Australian, Ron Grainer, and the Besier play, *The Barretts of Wimpole Street*, was being adapted by Ronald Millar. Martin Landau was the entrepreneur. Wendy enthused about all these people. She, of course, was going to direct it, and then she told me the other two divine pieces of news – one, that Sandy Faris was going to be the musical director, and two, that Malcolm Pride was going to be the designer. So there were four of us from the Sadler's Wells team back together again – Wendy, Sandy, Malcolm and June. Naturally I said I would love to be in it. After a couple of weeks, I had word from Wendy to say that the others were very excited about the fact that I was interested, that Ron Grainer had actually written the music with my voice in mind and that they would like to meet me as soon as possible.

Because of English tax law, I couldn't go back into England until after the financial year ended on 31 March. So we decided to meet in Paris. We arranged that we would all stay at a wonderful hotel called the Hotel Continental. I found out that it had actually been built by Napoleon as a townhouse for Josephine — it was some townhouse! Ron Millar, Ron Grainer and Martin Landau and I discussed the musical, and they told me all their ideas. That afternoon we went to the theatre where Ron Millar and Ron Grainer played and sang the score for me. The music was wonderful, the lyrics I thought were tremendous.

They decided that I would go that evening with Ron Grainer to a friend's house and work on two or three of the songs so that I could sing them for everybody the following day. I sang in the ballroom of the Hotel Continental. It was the most splendid place I've ever seen. I couldn't have thought of a more wonderful and fitting place for me to sing Ron Grainer's songs with Ron Millar's words to Martin Landau and Ron Miller. They said they were quite pleased, so I just kept my fingers crossed. We all had a marvellous luncheon and by then I was on complete and utter tenterhooks. After lunch Martin Landau said, 'Now, June, we'd like you to go upstairs and read some of the play with Ronnie Millar.' So we went to my suite, I read with Ronnie and he thanked me. I was still on tenterhooks, wondering what was going on. Still not a word had been said when we started our afternoon tea.

Suddenly Ronnie Millar took a great white handkerchief out of his pocket and blew his nose quite violently. I thought that was a bit rough over tea! But immediately Martin Landau said, 'It's yours, June.' I was excited and thrilled, but asked, 'Why have you kept me waiting all this time?'

Martin said, 'We were waiting for the signal. The signal was to come from Ronnie Millar. If he thought you were good enough after the reading, he'd blow his nose.' What a laugh we all had!

We started rehearsals in July 1964. They had assembled an absolutely superb cast. The boys who were playing my brothers were terrific performers themselves, and were completely right for the characters they were playing. My sisters, Henrietta and Arabel, couldn't have been better cast in a million years; every minor character was thought of—they had the right people to play the right parts, right down to the opening chorus scene—you couldn't have wished for anything better. And, of course, we had the most beautiful golden cocker spaniel playing Flush, Elizabeth's dog. It was a very happy company.

It was a hard grind, but it was fascinating to be associated for the first time in my career with a show that had never been performed before. We went through some great trials and tribulations with certain things. Sometimes I'd say to Ron Grainer that a certain phrase didn't sit quite right for me vocally and he'd rewrite it. Ron Grainer was very accommodating—he was wonderful. But we didn't have quite the same co-operation with Ronnie Millar. Wendy Toye would often say, 'Ronnie darling, I really do think that those words aren't quite right. Could we cut so and so and so and so?' And he'd say, 'No, Wendy, I've written those words and they're staying.' He was a darling person but once he had written something, that was that, and even if it was a difficult word to sing, he couldn't change it. So we had a few anxious moments in those early rehearsal days.

John Clements was splendidly cast as Edward Moulton-Barrett, my father. The man himself is a complete and utter disciplinarian, both on and off stage. I fell for Keith Michell straight away. He is handsome, tall and blond, with a beautiful speaking voice and a lovely singing voice—I was rather hooked on Michell!

During rehearsals, though, I discovered sometimes that he just didn't seem to be quite happy with what Wendy Toye would say. He'd say, 'Yes, I'll try it that way, Wendy,' but then he'd say, 'Do you think if I tried it like this?' and demonstrate. Of course, this absolutely amazed me, because in those days I just did what the director told me to do. (Now I'm more like the Keiths of the profession.) As the rehearsals progressed and we got closer to our out-of-town opening in Leeds, Keith still wasn't completely word-perfect. I was becoming a little worried. Ronnie Millar took me aside one day and said, 'June, don't take any notice of dear Keith. He's like that. He'll always let you think he doesn't quite know it and then walks out on the opening night, word-perfect, brilliant, and runs away with all the notices. Don't let him fluster you. Just think of your own performance.' Which I did. Ronnie was quite right, though. Keith was word-perfect and brilliant!

So we tropped up to Leeds and opened in September at the wonderful old Grand Theatre. If anything could go wrong on that opening night, it did! Sets wouldn't quite move, they wouldn't quite come together, they'd move forward slightly, they wouldn't revolve completely. The train left Victoria Station on a wrong cue and Keith and I were left stranded racing after the train – you name it, it happened. The curtain eventually came down, three and a quarter hours after curtain up, and we realised that a bit of cutting had to be done! We also thought that the audience couldn't wait to get out but they stayed and cheered. They wanted more, they didn't want to leave the theatre! It was a very exciting opening, even though so much did go wrong.

The following morning we decided the things that had to be cut and relearned for the performance that night. In the last act there was a beautiful duet which I sang with Keith, quite the loveliest piece of music in the entire show, we all thought, but it held up the action so it had to go. They decided to cut most of John Clement's songs because while he is a really fine actor, he is not a great singer. All sorts of changes happened. Then we had to go on for the second performance and try to remember all the cuts! It was still far too long, so out came the scissors again. Eventually we got the show down to two and a quarter hours. People just flocked to see it. It was the greatest success for many years.

One matinee in Leeds was on 12 September, the anniversary of Robert and Elizabeth's wedding. When Keith knelt at my feet (when I was in the wheelchair), begging me to marry him, he should have said, 'Elizabeth, I want you for my wife,' instead of which he said, 'Elizabeth, I want to be your wife.' He looked at me with horror on his face and said, 'Oh, my God.' Then he took me in a passionate embrace. We could hear the audience saying, 'Did he . . . say what I think he said?' etc. We were shaking with laughter!

After a performance one night I found a note at my hotel asking me to go to Mr Grainer's suite. I thought, 'Oh dear'—I always think the worst—'What have I done? What am I not doing right?' So in fear and trepidation I went to Ron's suite and they were all there—Ronnie Millar, Ron Grainer, Wendy Toye, Martin Landau and Sandy Faris. Ronnie Millar said, 'We've just realised, June, that because of the cutting of the duet with Keith, you have nothing to sing after the Soliloquy at the beginning of Act II, so Ron and I have just written a nice light, little coloratura song for you which you sing to your father in the big confrontation scene with him.' Ron Grainer played it and they both sang it for me. Well, I nearly fell over backwards because it was anything but a 'nice light little coloratura' thing! It was very dramatic, very high and not really coloratura. It was a song called 'Woman and Man' and it really was quite the most exciting minute and a half of music imaginable. So I started to learn it that night, at about half past eleven. We decided we'd put it in at Manchester, our next port of call before London. As I said, it was very high, dramatic and exciting, finishing on a top D—a pretty high note to sing eight times a week in such a dramatic context. I think it was about the most successful song in the whole show and the boys had written it in twenty minutes!

In Manchester the success of Leeds was duplicated. But one thing was nagging us. We still didn't have the right title for the show. In Leeds and Manchester it had been called *The Barretts and Mr Browning*, but we wanted a better title. Everybody put their thinking caps on and a couple of very funny ideas came up—for instance, *The Lady's Not for Browning* and another was *Flush on a Hot Tin Couch*! Eventually, I think it was Wendy Toye who came up with the lovely idea of it simply being called *Robert and Elizabeth*.

So at last it was London – 21 October 1964 – and what an opening night that was! London went berserk. The press hailed it, the audience just stamped and cheered and didn't want the show to finish. They all wanted to know what happened after we arrived in Florence! After the performance on opening night, Wendy Toye put on a marvellous party for us at her apartment and we all had a wonderful time. We were naturally waiting for the newspapers to come out with the notices. We were all very jubilant and standing around chatting. Somebody asked me what it was like working with Keith. Keith was standing with us. I said, just gagging, 'Absolutely wonderful, except when he spits.'

Keith said, 'I beg your pardon?'

I said, still joking, 'Well, you know, you spit when you're talking and singing.'

'All great actors spit.'

'Well, that let's me out, doesn't it, because I don't spit!' I could see that he was a bit upset, so I said, 'Oh, come off it. It's all right for you, love, you're doing the spitting, but what about me? I'm on the receiving end. I see it coming at me, I don't know whether to duck or let it land and then, after a while, wipe it off very surreptitiously.'

With that he stormed out of the room, into Wendy's study. I followed him, saying, 'Oh, Keith I'm sorry, I didn't mean to upset you, but it is a bit disconcerting when somebody spits at you.'

He turned on me and said, 'Let me tell you, your performance would be nothing without me!'

To which I replied, 'And let me tell you, your vocal performance would be nothing without me!'

Of course he was very upset. I was very upset. Then he grabbed his wife, Jenny, and they left the party. I apologised to Wendy for upsetting her party. I thought I couldn't talk to Keith again! Then Richard, my husband, said, 'The show is a great success and you are going to be working together for a very long time. One of you has to make the first move and I'd like it to be you.'

When I got into the theatre the next day, as I walked in the stage-door, Keith was signing in. He turned around and looked at me. We threw ourselves into each other's arms and said, almost simultaneously, 'We're a couple of temperamental Australians, aren't we?' And we've loved each other ever since.

While the show contained its long run, lots of funny things happened, both on stage and off, both in England and in Australia (where we evenually toured).

One day a friend of mine with a good voice said she'd like to audition for the understudy of my role, so I made arrangements for her to sing and read for the company and management. When she got there, she said, 'My friend told me to come along here. Her name is Mabel Brownlow.'

They said, 'We don't know anybody called Mabel Brownlow.'

'That's her real name, Mabel Brownlow. You probably know her as June Bronhill.'

So ever since then I have been known affectionately by all my dearest friends as Mabel, or Mabel Brownlow, to give the full fictitious title!

John Clements, as I said, was a strict disciplinarian. We all behaved ourselves when we were on stage with him. There was a lovely scene with Bella Hedley, our cousin, played delightfully by Sarah Badell, in which she was flirting outrageously with Papa. Eventually he pulled her on to his knees and kissed her quite passionately, then pulled himself together because the next scene was one with all the brothers and sisters — an important scene. He brushed her aside and he should have said, 'Run along now, child, I have to speak privately to my family.' At one performance, he brushed her aside and said, 'Run along now, child, I have to speak family to my privates.' He realised what he'd said and said, 'I mean, er . . .' and stuttered and stammered. Of course he only made it worse. We then had to come on stage. How we kept straight faces I'll never know. He was still quite flummoxed.

Instead of saying things like, 'We are leaving London and going to Bookham, Surrey, on Tuesday 14th,' he said something like, 'On Tuesday, 5th, no, 4th, we're leaving Book . . . no, we're leaving . . .' It was just hysterical!

At the end of Act I when Robert (Keith) eventually got Elizabeth up out of her wheelchair, and she was so excited because she had actually walked three steps, Papa entered and found them in each other's arms. Elizabeth said, 'Look, Papa, I can walk!' He was very cruel and reminded her of her dead brother. She was so shattered by his reaction that she fainted. Papa caught her, lifted her in his arms and ordered Browning from the house, saying, 'You must never come here again.' He then carried her back into the house and left Browning, centre stage. One night when I'd fainted, John (Papa) farted as he bent down to pick me up. I was supposed to be in a dead faint so I couldn't react. He carried me off stage, the curtain came down, he put me down and suddenly said, 'I'm sorry, must hurry. Got some people coming backstage. See you later,' and dashed off. Keith and I walked off stage together. We didn't say a word. When we got to our dressing-rooms, as one we put our heads out of the doors, looked at each other and said, 'He did, didn't he?'

In the second act, when Elizabeth was really walking again, she was looking out of her window when she saw Browning. He looked up and saw her on her feet. He came rushing into the house, up the staircase, into her bedroom and said, 'Want to be well and you've done it, you've won.' In one particular performance the trucks that were supposed to meet when I was standing at the window just couldn't meet, they couldn't be toggled. Every time they came together, they parted. It was really quite amusing, because we had lines to say that made the situation even funnier. For instance, when he entered my bedroom, I said, 'Robert, you shouldn't have come,' and he replied, 'If you think an earthquake could have kept me away!' and with that the whole thing just split miles apart, like an earthquake! The audience started to giggle a bit. Everything we did or said related to the fact that we really couldn't get together. We'd try to get together, we had to bound across this chasm, and I was terrified because the gown I wore had a train and I thought it would be my luck that the two trucks would come together at last and I'd be caught with my train firmly embedded between them! This went on for a good ten minutes with both the audience and ourselves in fits of laughter.

In the end Keith went over to the prompt corner and said, 'We've been doing this show for over 500 performances, so surely you can get it together by now.' They tried hard and eventually managed to get it together. Of course the audience loved this. Audiences adore things that go wrong – they realise we're just human after all! We were getting close to the following scene which I had with my father. Keith was kneeling at my feet; we and the audience were still laughing. Keith whispered to me, 'You've got this scene coming up now with John – I think we'd better pull ourselves together.' So we did. We both, as one, drew our hands down over our faces and became serious. The amazing thing was that the audience got the message and became serious as well.

Jeremy Lloyd, a brilliantly funny actor, was playing Captain Certes Cook who was in love with my sister, Henrietta. She brought Cook to meet me. He was in the Coldstream Guards and he wore his full-dress uniform, with the breastplate and helmet with the white plumes – the lot! We had a delightful scene together. At one performance, as he left he clicked his heels and put his helmet to his breastplate in the full military manner, and something went wrong. Suddenly, there were little screws and nuts and bolts from the breastplate falling all over the floor! The next scene I had was my first scene with Robert Browning. Elizabeth was very nervous about the fact that Browning was coming to visit her. When it was announced that he was downstairs, she started to pour some pills into her hand, wanting to take some to calm her down. While she did this, Browning opened the door very quietly and said, 'Miss Barrett.' She jumped to high heaven and pills went all over the place. The scene between them was quite delightful, with Browning picking up the pills and giving them back to Elizabeth, all the while saying lovely things about her and her poems. Well, this performance was a field day for Keith. He picked up little nuts, bolts, screws, pills and anything else he could find on the floor to put in my hand and I, of course, had to find somewhere to put them! He's a real devil, is that Michell!

The success of *Robert and Elizabeth* was something beyond everybody's dreams. It was packed to capacity at every performance; cables were sent from America to reserve seats. You couldn't get a seat for love nor money. I even used to get beautiful presents sent over from America – not for me, but for my daughter! They'd heard that I had a daughter so in their usual generous fashion they sent lovely dolls and books to her.

On the occasion of our 500th performance, I had a lovely surprise with a visit backstage from Kevin Coulsen, a fellow Australian performer I'd worked with a lot in television in Australia. Kevin had just arrived in London, was walking past the theatre, saw my name up there and thought, 'I must go round and see Bronhill.' We had a great chat and I asked him what he was doing. He said he didn't have any work, he'd only just arrived. I asked, 'Do you want to see the show?' He said he'd been to the box office but found it was absolutely booked out. I said, 'Leave it with me and we might be able to find you a seat. Also, tonight after the performance we're having our 500th party on stage, so come with me as my guest.' He said he'd love to.

I managed to get him a seat and, after the show, Kevin was absolutely in raptures about it. Now, Kevin is very tall, good-looking, a lovely singer, a lovely actor, and at the party everybody was asking me, 'Who's the dishy bloke?'

Martin Landau asked me, 'Who's your friend?'

'A very good young performer from Australia.'

'Does he sing?'

'Yes, he does. Why?'

'Well, you know Keith's got his holidays coming up soon and we really are looking for somebody to take over his role.'

'Well, I'm sure Kevin would love to audition for you.'

So it was arranged that Kevin would audition. Not only was he accepted as Keith's replacement during his holiday but also they asked if he would take over from Keith when he left the show about four months later. So Kevin Coulsen, by walking past the Lyric Theatre that night, just fell on his feet in the West End of London – with me helping him!

Keith Michell was the first of the original cast to leave the show. For his last matinee performance he came up with the idea of going on stage in a disguise at various odd times. On top of his costume he had on a great long overcoat and a real old bushie's hat, dragged down over his head so the audience really couldn't guess it was Keith. He really was hysterical. He would appear at the most unexpected times. For instance, in the opening scene, where a little bar in a pub came on stage with some of the prostitutes propping it up, there was Keith playing up to them! In the garden scene when I was out of doors for the first time in my wheelchair, someone whispered, 'Have a look over your shoulder,' and there he was, peering round a tree at the back of the garden wall, waving to me in funny little gloves with torn and flapping fingers. Next he appeared almost immediately before he had to go on in the Vauxhall Gardens scene, where he sings the beautiful song, 'Escape Me Never'! This ever-recurring figure going through all the scenes was amazing. We all thought it was delightful, very funny, but would you believe, the stage management hauled him over the coals! We all thought he was brilliant and he hadn't upset the show in any way.

Next I was told that John Clements would be leaving quite soon and that his role as Edward Moulton-Barrett was being taken over by Sir Donald Wolfitt. Naturally it was very exciting for me to perform with another great actor. The problem, though, was that I was rehearsing during the day

111

with Wolfitt and performing at night with Clements, and they were entirely different in their reading of the role. The parts that John Clements would play in a dark manner, Wolfitt would do in a quick, high, offhand manner; the converse happening nearly all the time. I didn't know whether I was coming or going! I was quite exhausted at this stage, too. When Wolfitt had agreed to do the role, he agreed on condition that I played Elizabeth opposite him for three months. That was impossible because of the impending Australian tour; I could only do it for three weeks. The management thought that Wolfitt would say he wouldn't do it but he said three weeks was better than nothing, which I thought was rather lovely of him.

Wolfitt was a darling, and he did lovely, sweet things. For instance, nearly every matinee day, he would come in with an egg for me. He'd tell me that it was a new-laid egg, fresh that morning from his and his wife's farm. It was almost as if it were still rationing days and a fresh egg was something really fantastic. But I treasured those eggs and always had a boiled new-laid egg for breakfast the morning after the matinee, thanks to dear Sir Donald. On my last London performance, 4 April 1966, he presented me with a lovely last-night present which was a marvellous bronze theatrical medallion, with a large green stone set in it, which he told me had belonged to Sir David Garrick. He said he had worn it as Richard III. I've treasured it ever since.

It really was quite the most extraordinary closing night for me. I had been with the show for nineteen months, and apart my short holiday, I'd only missed four performances. Everybody gave me the most beautiful presents, lovely things that I will always treasure.

During those last few weeks, I had discovered that I was having a bit of trouble with my throat. I was not singing as well in certain parts of my voice as I knew I should be, and I was coughing a lot. My speaking voice off stage was very husky and I felt that I was very tired — after all, I was at the end of a nineteen-month season of eight performances a week, which is a lot of singing! But I thought a few days in Honolulu on the way to Australia and a couple of days rest when I got to Sydney and I would be all right. But it wasn't to be, was it! We flew to Honolulu and had five days there during which my throat became steadily worse. When I eventually arrived in Australia I knew that there was something very wrong with me.

We arrived in Sydney at about 7.30 in the morning and I was met by my dear singing teacher, Madame Mathy, who had arrived with a couple of bottles of chilled champagne. A couple of other friends and quite a barrage of press also met me. I skilfully hid my husky voice and carried it off well. The following day there was a big welcoming party to meet the Australian cast. My Robert was a wonderful English actor, Dennis Quilley, and my father was a man we all love dearly, Frank Thring, a marvellous actor and a wonderful character. Halfway through the cocktail party, my throat was really getting very bad. I said to Richard that I thought I should go back to the hotel and not talk any more. My voice was really very husky indeed. John Carroll, of Garnet Carroll Productions, who were putting on the show, made an appointment for me to see Melbourne's top throat specialist the following morning. The specialist said I definitely had a nodule, something all singers are terrified of getting. He was an elderly gentleman and he said, 'I'm too old to do the operation and I wouldn't know who to recommend. All I can suggest is that you just keep quiet—you don't speak for four weeks.' I thanked him and left. I said to Richard, 'Well, the show *opens* in four weeks, so how am I not going to rehearse?' Then I decided to phone dear old Madame Mathy to see if she could suggest anything.

She told me to come up to Sydney straightaway because she had a wonderful throat specialist, Dr Barat, whom she would recommend to anybody. I flew to Sydney and saw Dr Barat that night. He said that he could remove my nodule, but that it was a tricky operation. If the chord was nicked by just the slightest misplacement of the instrument, there

113

would be no voice left. I discussed it with Richard and Mathy and we decided that we would risk it.

The following morning, while I was under local anaesthetic, Dr Barat put an incredibly fine instrument down my throat. Then, very gently, he pulled it out and said, 'Put out your hand.' I did and he put a little grey ball that looked exactly like a Beluga caviar egg in it. He said (in his wonderful Hungarian accent), 'Now, you do not speak for one week, you just write everything down, you then can whisper very, very softly for one week, the third week you can start speaking but very quietly, and on the fourth week you can start singing and you will be all right for your opening night.' So I nodded. He said, 'Now, I want you to come to me tomorrow morning and I just have a look and see how it is healing.'

The following morning I wrote a note to a taxi driver and went to see Dr Barat again. He looked down my throat and said, 'It is a miracle. If I had not known that you had a nodule yesterday, I wouldn't be able to tell where it was; it has healed very quickly. Now you can start whispering for a few days, then you can start speaking. You can sing in ten days' time.'

I can't tell you what it was like when I opened my mouth to sing for the first time in about three weeks and to hear that I *could* sing! There were no croaks, no scratchy sounds. The voice was back, thanks to Dr Barat.

Once again, we had a splendid cast for *Robert and Elizabeth*, and our opening night was something that I don't think I'll ever forget. The outside of the Princess Theatre had been made to look like London's Wimpole Street. All along the walls were wonderful old carriage lamps; the fan lights were lit up beautifully; the inside of the theatre was red-carpeted everywhere; and up the marble staircase were the flowers which would be presented to us on stage at the end of the performance. It was just like a florist's shop or a garden – quite magnificent! And inside the auditorium every seat had a little bottle of 4711 Eau de Cologne, because of the song, 'Pass the Eau de Cologne for God's Sake'. There were also a little bunch of violets for the women and a carnation for the men, for their lapels. The theatre had been gently sprayed with eau de cologne and the whole effect was really quite beautiful! They certainly knew how to do things in those days!

The opening night was a sensation. I don't think they'd seen anything like it in Australia for a long while. Of all those beautiful bouquets up the staircase, twenty-two of them, would you believe, were for me! I had nowhere to put them all at home, so I got in touch with all the hospitals the following morning and some nurses came over to collect about eighteen or nineteen of them.

Frank Thring was playing my father. He's a marvellous character and a great actor. At every performance I used to wear a beautiful ring. It was a black opal, surrounded by diamonds. It sounds flashy, but it wasn't. At one matinee performance, I had just returned from a morning press function, and I didn't wear the black opal but another lovely ring, an amethyst surrounded by pearls and diamonds. So I thought I'd wear that on stage. In our first scene, Thring took one look at my hand and was suddenly reduced to laughter. Offstage I asked, 'What was so funny?'

'It was just suddenly noticing that you didn't have the opal on. It just seemed so strange and I couldn't help laughing.'

I thought, 'Right! Every so often, at a matinee, I'll do something silly with the ring situation and just see what his reation is.'

The first thing I did was get some of those awful big pearls you buy at Woolies with great big holes that you thread through. I threaded it on string and tied it underneath my finger. When he looked down, he couldn't believe what he saw. After that, at each performance he'd look down to see what I had on my finger. I'd lull him into a sense of false security and then do another. Next I put a Bandaid around my finger and on the top of it, I put a bit of glue and stuck red glitter all over it. Once again he went completely sky-high. I did all sorts of evil things and he got to the stage where, even if I didn't do anything silly, he still had the giggles!

Charlton Heston happened to be visiting Melbourne during our season. Frank had appeared with him in many epics like *Ben Hur*, so lovely Thring decided he would give a party after the performance for the company to meet Charlton Heston. He was really quite splendid, very handsome and wonderful to meet, and it was a great thrill for all of us. As far as I was concerned, however, the big attraction of the night was the fact that the conductor, Dobbs Franks, was another guest. I had heard a tremendous amount about him but had never met him. I absolutely swooned over Dobbs Franks! I sat at his feet nearly all night, listening to every word he said in his Milwaukee accent, which was hard for me to understand. I was out of my mind, just sitting there knocking back a few drinks and having a wonderful time. I said to my husband, 'Don't worry about me, I'm not coming home. I'm walking out of the show. I'm going to Bangkok tomorrow morning with Dobbs.' Of course this was not true but I just thought it would be wonderful. Eventually I got home at about 6.30 in the morning, had about three or four hours sleep, then had to go in for the matinee! I was still on a high of excitement but I didn't realise it was also the alcohol in me! In my first scene, the dialogue was fine but when it came to singing, my co-ordination of music and words, for the first time in my life, was a little haywire. A large dose of Vitamin B soon put that right, I'm happy to say!

At another matinee, at the beginning of Act II when Elizabeth was back in her room once more on her chaise-longue, with Papa standing over her making her drink a tankard of porter, because he thought it was the best thing for her health, Frank Thring put the tankard into my hand and I was just about to drink this dreadful stuff when a male voice from the front row of the stalls said, 'Oh, he's got her back on the beer again!' in the broadest Australian accent you've ever heard! How we managed to carry on with the show I don't know.

The show was a fantastic success in Melbourne. We played to capacity houses for seven and a half months before moving on to Sydney. Before going to Sydney I took a day off and flew up to find an apartment to live in while we did the show in Sydney. I went to my favourite estate agent in Double Bay and on the way I passed the dear old Tivoli Theatre. There wasn't a sign outside to say that we were opening in a fortnight's time. There wasn't even a poster. I couldn't believe it. When I got to the estate agent, they asked me what I was doing in Sydney.

'Well, I'm opening in a fortnight at the Tivoli Theatre in *Robert and Elizabeth.*'

'But there's been no publicity. We haven't seen or heard anything. Everybody thinks that the old Tiv's closed because they had a closing-down gala night recently with everybody weeping and wailing because it was the end of the old Tivoli—it was being pulled down. This was about a month or so ago, and everybody thinks that's it.'

'Well, it isn't it. We'll be there in a fortnight.'

I flew back to Melbourne and told everybody, including John Carroll, all of this. John said, 'Oh, it's OK. It'll all be OK,' which of course it wasn't. The people who came to see the show absolutely loved it. This was also just before Christmas, which was not a good time to open a show without a lot of pre-publicity. Consequently we only lasted five weeks in Sydney, which was ridiculous. When the 'last two weeks' notices appeared in the newspapers and on the boards outside the theatre, people just flocked to it! People still hadn't known it was on. How sad that we closed! I'm sure there was an enormous Sydney audience deprived of seeing a great show, *Robert and Elizabeth.*

At our last performance I made my usual final solo curtain call, walking down centre stage with Flush, my dog. I was standing there, smiling and bowing, when suddenly Flush started doing that extraordinary thing that dogs do.

You know, going in little circles and getting faster and faster. Then she sat down with her back to the audience and did, well, one of the biggest jobs in the business! The audience fell about, the curtain came down, stage-hands came from all over the place to clean it up! I had to make a final curtain speech and I assured the audience that Flush's reaction had nothing whatsoever to do with *our* feelings about the show closing so early – it was just her own comment!

During the Australian run I had word from London to say that negotiations had gone through for us to do *Robert and Elizabeth* on Broadway. Keith Michell would be doing it with me but John Clements wasn't available and Rupert Davies, of Maigret fame, would be playing Edward Moulton-Barrett. It was all very exciting. Money had been discussed; when we would start rehearsals had been discussed; contracts were ready to be signed; I'd given up my apartments in London and in Melbourne, and I was due to leave in about ten days time. I was going to fly via the South of France and have a holiday there, visit a few friends in London and then go off to America. Then I had a cable to say that the American production had been cancelled because of a dispute over the American rights. The case was eventually thrown out of court, but the show never did get to Broadway.

I had to find work quickly because I had thought we'd be on Broadway for a year, if not longer. And something quite different turned up for me. I was asked to perform at a nightclub in Melbourne called the Lido, an elegant club – which had some topless girls in it! I was asked to be their guest artist for four weeks – not topless, I assure you! But I did have a marvellous photograph taken for the press. I was very demure and prim and proper in a little pink dress, covered up to my neck and with sleeves down to my wrists, surrounded by the topless girls. Wowee!

After I finished at the Lido I was asked to sing at another club, which was just opening in Adelaide, called the Celebrity Club. While I was there I had another cable from England asking me to play the role of Maria in *The Dancing*

Years by Ivor Novello. I was very excited about it because I had sung a lot of Ivor Novello's songs in the past but had never played in any of his musical comedies. So it was back to London for June.

10

The Dancing Years

When I returned to London after doing *Robert and Elizabeth* in Australia I immediately made an appointment to see Tom Arnold, the entrepreneur putting on *The Dancing Years*. Actually the rights of *The Dancing Years* belonged to his son, young Tom Arnold, who, if my memory serves me right, was Ivor Novello's godson. Ivor had left the rights to the show to young Tom. It was wonderful to meet this terrific man of the theatre. We had great chats about the show and about what he was planning to do with it. The plan actually was an extensive twelve-week tour of the provinces, with a very good prospect of it coming into the West End of London. I was highly delighted about all this. Before I left Australia I had managed to get hold of a score of *The Dancing Years* and I had worked on it with Madame Mathy. She had given me some good vocal ideas which were quite lovely and which made the music even lovelier.

We started rehearsals. A marvellous cast had been assembled. Rudi, the non-singing role that Ivor Novello created for himself, was a wonderful Canadian actor called David Knight, who was very tall, good-looking and charming. We had a marvellous Italian tenor, Enrico Giacomini, playing the role of the opera singer who sings in the operetta scene with me – a magnificent and moving voice, naturally very Italianate. During the run we had two Gretes, both enchanting actress–singer–dancers called Wendy Bowman and Cathy Jose. Moyna Cope, who was playing my singing teacher, Cacille Kurt, became a very good friend of mine. I had never met her before. She was quite lovely, with a wonderful mezzo soprano voice, a wonderful flair for the stage and a nice sense of comedy. We were put

Camping it up at a party in London, 1961 (*left to right*): Wendy Toye, Anna Pollak and June Bronhill.

A scene from *The Cunning Little Vixen* with June Bronhill (*left*) as the Vixen and Kevin Miller as the Fox.

June as Maria in the Australian production of *The Sound of Music*.

Richard Finny and June with their newborn daughter, Carolyn Jane, in Melbourne, 1963.

June as Elizabeth Barrett with her dog, Flush, in the London production of *Robert and Elizabeth* (1964).

June with Keith Michell (playing Robert Browning) in *Robert and Elizabeth*.

June and Keith Michell, with Edward Moulton-Barrett (a descendant of Elizabeth Barrett Browning), laying a wreath on Robert Browning's tomb in Poet's Corner, Westminster Abbey.

A portrait of June in costume for the Ivor Novello show, *The Dancing Years*.

through our paces by a wonderful director, Joan Davis, who was also our choreographer. Joan had worked on a number of the Ivor shows in past years—productions that Ivor had actually presented himself—as assistant choreographer and sometimes as choreographer, so we felt we were well looked-after in that respect.

To start with we rehearsed in the dress-circle bar of the Theatre Royal, Drury Lane. Everything went along swimmingly and we were loving the show. Of course, the other lovely thing for me was that, like so many of Ivor's shows, the lyrics and the book were written by that very dear friend of mine from *Merry Widow* days, Christopher Hassell. We changed a few things to make the words seem more acceptable in present-day language but otherwise we did it exactly as it was written. We did leave out the last scene which was like an epilogue set in Nazi Germany because we preferred it without. This disappointed a lot of people, but deep down I was happy that we left this scene out.

It was January and bitterly cold. During rehearsals I used to wrap myself up in big sweaters and furs to keep warm. After we'd been rehearsing for about two weeks, one day I suddenly felt a tap on my shoulder. I turned around but there was nobody there so I thought I'd imagined it. A while later, tap-tap on the shoulder again. I turned around, still nobody there, so I said, 'Now come on, which one of you so-and-sos is playing tricks on me and tapping me on the shoulder?' They all looked at me as if I were an idiot, not knowing what I was on about. This went on for about three or four days. Finally I said, 'I still can't believe that nobody is tapping me on the shoulder because I can even sometimes feel somebody pulling me around.'

They said, 'Oh, it's probably Ivor's ghost.'

'What do you mean?'

They explained that so many of his wonderful shows had been performed at the Theatre Royal, Drury Lane, and that his ghost is supposed to walk in the dress-circle bar area, where we rehearsed. So I don't know whether Ivor was there or not, but I've got a feeling that he was.

We eventually got the show together. I had nine costume changes and I had the most wonderful costume made for me. They were quite different from anything I'd ever worn before. Not showpiece gowns as I'd had in *The Merry Widow*, *Orpheus of the Underworld* or *La Vie parisienne*, but elegant creations from the 1920s and 1930s. I really felt a million dollars in them.

On tour around England, Scotland and Wales, we visited all the major cities. Everywhere we went, we played to capacity business. The audiences adored it, and eventually we were told that we were going into the West End of London. As a result, the sets were all revamped and the costumes were remade. The girls got new costumes, and mine were spruced up to look new. We moved into the Saville Theatre in Shaftesbury Avenue.

The opening night was yet another one of those incredible nights that you dream about. My role was Maria Zeigler, an operetta star. The show opens about five or six o'clock in the morning and all the girls from the show have been out gallivanting and partying with soldiers from a regiment which is passing through the town where they'd been performing. They arrived at an open-air café to have breakfast. They have all arrived on stage but Maria – she's obviously paying off the cabbies! Rudi, who works at the café, had his grand piano out in the courtyard. He sits down and starts playing. Maria heard the lovely music and, offstage, she started la-la-laing with him. Before I'd even put a foot on the stage on that opening night, the audience had started applauding wildly. This was the first time I'd appeared on the West End stage since *Robert and Elizabeth* and they gave me the most wonderful welcome back that you could ever wish to hear. They applauded and applauded and eventually I had to stop them with my hand up in the air so that we could get on with the play. My first line was 'I'll give you a thousand kronen for that waltz' – what a wonderful line to start with! I eventually paid him for the

waltz and it became mine. I sang the song right through –
'Waltz of My Heart' – and, would you believe, once again
they just cheered and stamped and carried on. Once again
I had to stop them so that we could get on with the show!
It was like this all night – everything we did just stopped the
show. It was incredible. Then, in the final curtain calls, they
went mad and they must have applauded for at least fifteen
minutes. I've never heard anything like that in my life. When
we came off the stage we were absolutely agog with
excitement. I turned to the company and said, 'We are here
for at least two years.' We all felt that way. The press was
wonderful; everybody adored it.

During our first two weeks you couldn't get a seat for
love nor money. The theatre was jam-packed – they were
hanging from the rafters. Then two awful things happened:
first, there was a heatwave in London (that's almost
unbelievable!) and second, there was a rail strike and business
just absolutely slumped. We had fairly good houses but not
the capacity ones we'd been having, and, after three weeks,
our two weeks notice was put up because if you didn't take
£5,000 for two weeks running, the theatre owners had the
right to give the company notice. One week I believe we took
about £4,800 and the other was about £4,500, and because
of that small difference we were given our marching orders.
Tom Arnold decided he was not going to be beaten; he would
give the company a couple of weeks holiday and then we
would go out on tour again, doing two weeks in Nottingham,
two weeks in Bristol, two weeks in Coventry, two weeks in
Oxford and then, he hoped, come back into the West End.

However, a few things went wrong. I began to have
trouble with a tumour on my pituitary gland, so I was taken
out of the show at Nottingham and taken down to hospital
in London to have special X-rays. My place was taken by
Jean Bayliss. They finished the two weeks in Nottingham,
went over to Bristol and after the two weeks were finished
there, a lot of the gang in the company decided they would
leave after the show on Saturday night, have Sunday at home

123

in London, then drive up to Coventry on the Monday. In one of the cars were five of the boys, including Enrico Giacomini. They were actually outside Ivor Novello's house, Redroofs, at Reading when a car came round the corner on the wrong side of the road and ran straight into our boys' car head-on. Enrico and the driver, and the other driver, were all killed. The other three were quite badly injured. When I found out about this, while I was in hospital, it seemed to me that Ivor had tapped me on the shoulder at rehearsals and was trying to tell me that something was wrong, something bad was going to happen with this show, and that we should stop doing it—it was never meant to be.

They only did a week in Coventry. Enrico's understudy took over, but everybody felt that the show had the kiss of death upon it. They were worried about me and didn't know what was going to happen to me; Enrico was killed; Keith (the driver) was killed; the other three boys were badly hurt and in a tremendous state of shock. Another dreadful thing happened during that tour. David Knight had told us that his wife was pregnant and they were both very excited. Then, when they discovered that his wife was going to have twins, they were even more excited. During our short London season, one twin was stillborn and the one that survived was mongoloid.

What had started out as a most exciting project had become such a sad time for everyone.

In 1970, after the South African tour of *Robert and Elizabeth*, I was asked by Peter Bridge, of Alexander Bridge Productions, if I would be interested in playing the role of Sari in a provincial tour of Noël Coward's *Bitter Sweet*. I just jumped at it! I was thrilled to bits because I had been such a fan of Coward's for so long. We had gathered a lovely cast. The role of Carl was played by John Larsen who had been my Danilo when I first came home to Australia in 1960 in *The Merry Widow*. A wonderful actor called John Marsden played the villain of the piece who eventually kills Carl in a sword fight at the end of Act II. I had some beautiful

124

costumes designed by Alan Sievewright. The production was really put together very well. Peter Bridge himself directed. His company was a touring company; he had done some successful productions in Southend-on-Sea and Westcliffe in Essex but I think this was the first time he'd done an extensive provincial tour. His mother, Eileen Farrow, was generally in Peter's productions – you know the old saying, keep it in the family. She was playing Manon, the beautiful role created by Ivy St Helier when Coward originally put on the show.

The wonderful thing about the role of Sari is that she starts as a woman of seventy, then reminisces about her youth to some young people at a party she is giving. So from seventy she goes very quickly – a thirty- to forty-second costume and wig change – to a seventeen-year-old girl. During the acts she changes from seventeen to twenty-five to forty and then back to seventy at the end. It's really quite a *tour-de-force* for a performer. I wondered how I was going to manage this aging process. One night I was in one of my favourite restaurants in Soho in London, the Rigoletto, and who should be in there but Evelyn Laye who had played Sari on Broadway in 1929 and London in 1930. We were thrilled to see each other. I said, 'Now, come on, Boo, you can help me. I'm doing *Bitter Sweet* and I'm wondering how you managed to do that quick change from the elderly woman to the young girl.'

'Well, naturally, June, you don't have time to change make-up. I had a slight hump built into my costume as the old woman, to give a round-shouldered look. But I don't think it was really necessary – I think it's all in the thought process and the way you use your speaking voice. Just slow down your speaking voice and make it a little mellow . . . you know, how elderly people speak – a little bit like the way I speak now. And with a slight stoop and a gentle clouding of the face, not being quite so alive – you can then create it. In a split second you can take off the grey wig, put on the young wig, get into a young costume and just by facial expression, vocal expression and the way you use your body, you will shed forty years.'

So I took her advice and it worked magically.

The tour was a great success and we were thrilled with the reaction. We would have loved to have done a West End season but that, unfortunately, wasn't forthcoming. The closest we got to the West End was a week in Croydon and a week at Wimbledon, both places having a beautiful theatre. After our week in Wimbledon, we had a week out before going to Liverpool for a week and after that I was taking six weeks out of the production to go to Australia to do some work which had been pre-organised some time before.

On the Saturday night of our week out, I tripped on a step and tore all the ligaments in my foot. The doctor told me not to walk on it. I explained that I had to perform that week and the doctor said, 'Well, they'll have to put your understudy on.' I told Peter Bridge all this, and he replied, 'Your understudy basically knows the role but she hasn't any costumes and she's not really fully prepared.' Of course she couldn't wear my costumes because she was five foot seven and I'm four foot eleven! So I had to do that week in Liverpool!

In the first scene where I was elderly, I did it on a wheelchair; in some scenes I was able to do it on crutches, in other scenes I was able to use a walking-stick and in some of the scenes, some of the boys carried me on and off. However, there was one scene in which none of these things could happen. It was a scene with my mother, an elegant suitor and myself, and I had to go off the stage alone, in a slight temper. I couldn't use the crutches or walking stick because in this particular scene I was the young girl, so I hopped off! The audience was absolutely marvellous. I expected them to shriek with laughter but they didn't – they were so understanding.

Peter Bridge was so thrilled with the success of *Bitter Sweet* that he asked me if I would do another provincial tour for him in 1971, this time an Ivor Novello musical,

Glamorous Night. I was thrilled because I had enjoyed working in *The Dancing Years* so much. It was a similar cast to that of *Bitter Sweet* except that, because it was an Ivor Novello musical, the leading man didn't sing. At the first rehearsal I met my new leading man. He was the prettiest boy imaginable – young enough to be my son, camp as Chloe, and dressed exquisitely in white and cream. I put up with him mincing around the rehearsal room for about ten days until, one day, I realised it was just ludicrous; that I was going to look stupid on stage with this boy. We started rehearsing a scene together where we were lost in the desert. We were exhausted and supposed to sit down in the sand and try to get our bearings. That day he was wearing white trousers and a white sweater and looking so pretty and lovely. Naturally he didn't sit down on the floor, he just squatted down, and said his lines very tweely. Suddenly I just couldn't take any more. I said, 'Are you going to sit down as you're supposed to or aren't you?'

'Oh, but I've got my lovely white flannels on.'

'You shouldn't wear your lovely white flannels to rehearsal – you should come in rehearsal clothes. I'm just fed up with this whole thing!' And I turned to Peter and said, 'Make up your mind, Peter – either he goes or I go,' and I walked out, something I've never done before or since.

Poor Peter didn't know what to do with himself. I just went and sat in the green room. After about fifteen minutes Peter found me and said, 'I'm dreadfully sorry, June. I just thought he'd be all right.'

'Well, I'm sorry too, Peter, but I cannot subject myself to this sort of thing.'

'Don't worry, June. The minute you'd left the room, he came up to me and said, "I'm so glad June doesn't want me because I don't think I'm right for the part in any case." So it's all worked out for the best.'

The actor who took over was Paul Greenhalgh, who was enchanting and just exactly right for the role. And he became one of my dearest friends.

Glamorous Night was again a great success. It looked elegant. Peter Bridge really did things very well. During *Glamorous Night* I met a wonderful woman who had been in nearly all of Ivor Novello's shows, Olive Gilbert — what a darling woman. She was then about seventy but she still sang like a dream. Many times when she sang 'Shanty Town' in Act II it brought tears to my eyes. She was a sweetheart and we remained friends until she died a few years ago.

In this musical, the heroine was once again an opera singer but she was of gypsy extraction. When she was lost with the leading man in the desert, she suddenly heard gypsy music which led them to a gypsy encampment. By then, of course, the couple were in love and so they decided to get married by gypsy law. It was staged quite beautifully. All the gypsy ladies formed a double line going down to the centre front stage from upstage right, and the gypsy men did the converse on the opposite side. I walked down through the gypsy girls, and Paul would walk down through the gypsy men. Standing centre front, with their backs to the audience, were Eileen Farrow, who was playing the gypsy priestess, and a dear friend of mine, John Aron, who was playing the gypsy priest. Part of John's costume was a wonderful, great big gypsy medallion on a chain around his neck.

One particular performance, as I walked through the gypsy girls, I could see that they were giggling at something and trying desperately not to smile. I muttered, 'What's going on?' They said, 'Look at John.' Paul and I were walking down and gazed into each other's eyes across the stage and we met in front of the gypsy priest and priestess. We turned to them and there I saw that, instead of his beautiful, great gold gypsy medallion, John had a Bronnley's lemon soap on a rope around his neck! How we got through that wedding scene, with us giving our wrists to be cut and the blood being joined and the handkerchief tied around them, I will never, ever know.

When I came off stage Eileen said, 'What was you all laughin' about?' (She had quite a Cockney accent.)

I said, 'Didn't you see John? He didn't have his proper medallion on – he had a Bronnley's lemon soap on a rope.'

Eileen said, 'Ho, no, Hai was completely hinto mai part. You see, Hai was playin' a gypsy priestess and Haim halways what Haim playing and Hai was playin' a gypsy priestess so Hai *was* a gypsy priestess.'

Biggest load of trash I've ever heard, and all in one of those awful put-on posh voices!

Because of the success of *Glamorous Night* in 1971, Peter wanted me to do another Ivor Novello in 1972. Once again I agreed. This one was going to be *Perchance to Dream* and again with dear Paul Greenhalgh as the male lead. However, I said to Peter that I would only do this one if his mother wasn't in it, because while she was a dear, she really wasn't all that good. She was rather amateursville and everything else about the productions had been professional. Peter appeared in these shows as well and was wonderful; outrageous, flamboyant but a great performer. He agreed with me and was quite happy to leave Mother out.

We finished rehearsals and everything had gone marvellously. We had lovely Olive Gilbert again, playing what I suppose would have been played by Mother. We were opening in Eastbourne at a matinee. It was bitterly cold, with heavy snow falling. I was settling into my dressing-room when suddenly there was a great panic. Olive had slipped in the snow and twisted her hip. The curtain was going up in an hour and a half. What were we going to do? Would you believe, Mother was in the pub across the road, where we were all staying! She'd come down to Eastbourne for the week, she knew the role and she knew every move. She took over. So I had Mother on stage with me after all. Olive was only off for that week so it wasn't too bad. We all decided that Mother and Peter had sat down and discussed the whole thing and, knowing that Olive was no longer young, they had probably thought they'd better have something up their sleeves, just in case! Eileen had all the moves down pat. It was just as if she had been rehearsing with us all along.

Perchance to Dream was a great success. Unfortunately it was the last of the lovely Ivor Novello shows I did. I've always been very grateful to Peter Bridge and his company for giving me the opportunity to perform in two Ivor Novello shows and of course to be involved with that lovely Noël Coward masterpiece, *Bitter Sweet*.

Some years later in Australia in 1978, three friends and I came up with the idea of putting together a show using the words and music of Ivor Novello and Noël Coward. We decided to call it *The Masters* and we had great fun with it. It was interesting doing the research and finding out amazing things about these two great men of the theatre. They had been close friends, with a terrific admiration for each other. The other people involved were Dennis Olsen, an actor, singer and a pianist of concert class; Brian Crossley, a director with whom I'd worked before, a wonderful, bubbly, effervescent chap who, like all of us, loved both Coward and Novello; Rex Wrennall, a very dear friend, whom I'd met at the Sydney Opera House; and Freddie Phillips, our musical director. Freddie Phillips was another very dear friend of mine who had played for me on numerous occasions at concerts – and parties! – throughout Australia. Freddie was one of those marvellous pianists who could transpose at the drop of a hat. Sadly, he died a few years ago.

Together we sat and thought and worked and devised, and between us we put together this gem of a show. We set it in a simple elegant drawing-room with two grand pianos, one for Dennis and one for Freddie.

There was a lovely song sung by Dennis Olsen in the Coward Section called 'Auntie Jessie'. On our opening night in Melbourne, Dennis started singing, 'We must all be very kind to Auntie Jessie/For she's never been a mother or a wife,/You mustn't throw your toys at her . . .' and he stopped. He didn't know what came next. He turned to me and asked, 'What comes next?'

'I don't know, she's not *my* Auntie Jessie,' I said.

We played in Melbourne, Sydney, Adelaide, Canberra,

Hobart, Launceston and Burnie. Everywhere we went people absolutely loved it. I hope one day I have the chance to do it again.

11

Variety is the Spice of Life

Having conquered the worlds of opera, operetta and musical comedy, most sopranos would have been satisfied – but not Bronhill. Variety is the spice of life and do I love life!

In my early days at Sadler's Wells I was asked to sing at lots of Sunday concerts around England and in Wales. I have lots of lovely memories of the ones in Wales in particular. These were generally Sunday concerts where one sang for about ten minutes in each half. The rest of the concert was the local choir and a local artist. There's nothing like a wonderful Welsh choir even though they may be just a local choir. I would travel by train, leaving London in the morning, arriving wherever the concert was, somewhere in the Rhondda Valley, at Llanelli or Llandudno or Ilfracombe or wherever, in mid-afternoon. I would be met by the choirmaster and taken to the rehearsal. The choir generally had rehearsed already and I'd think, 'Oh, they'll go and let me rehearse on my own,' but oh, no, they had to sit and listen.

At one particular concert, just before I started to rehearse my first aria, one of the members of the choir said to me in a lovely Welsh accent, 'You'll have to be very good, because last concert we had that Betty Fretwell here. Oh, what a beautiful voice she's got! You'll have to be very good to be as good as she was.' So before I'd even opened my mouth, I was in fear and trepidation that I wasn't going to be as good as Elizabeth Fretwell or Victoria Elliott or Amy Shuard, or whoever might have sung there before! At one, I'm happy to say they did say to me, 'You'll be all right, girl, we like you, you'll do, you're OK!'

Invariably the accompanist was the wife of the

132

choirmaster, a Mrs Evans, a Mrs Davis or a Mrs Thomas and while she was never really a great pianist, she got by. Once at a concert in a wonderful little church hall, when I was singing an aria from *The Daughter of the Regiment*, Mrs Thomas turned the first page with such vigour that the whole musical score collapsed in a mangled heap! There were sheets of music all over the floor. We had to stop while we picked it all up and got it into order again so we could start once more. She was a wonderful one, that Mrs Thomas. She took it all in her stride with a laugh.

At one marvellous concert I did in Wales, I was guest artist for the Tredegar Orpheus Male Voice Choir, a choir with 150 wonderful Welsh voices. The venue where we were performing seated 850 and it was packed out. When it came to my final song, which was 'The Holy City', I said to everyone, audience and choir, that I wanted them all to join in the Jerusalem refrains. They did and it was electrifying! Nobody, anywhere in the world, can harmonise like the Welsh, and to hear a thousand Welsh voices raised in song, in magnificent song, is something that will live with me forever.

After I finished my career with Sadler's Wells, and in between my other commitments, I did lots of concert tours around the provinces of England, Scotland and Wales. These I loved doing because they were generally 'An Evening with June Bronhill and Friends'. I would have a male singer with me, so we could do some lovely duets, and there would be a pianist and an organist. They were super, fun concerts and I enjoyed them particularly because one reached more members of the public. When we did our Sadler's Wells opera tours, I discovered that there were a lot of people who didn't want to sit through a whole opera but would love to to go a concert where they could hear a little bit of opera, operetta, musical comedy, lovely songs by Ivor Novello and Noël Coward, old-time songs like 'Danny Boy' and 'Smilin' Through' and lovely religious songs like the Bach-Gounod 'Ave Maria' and 'The Holy City' – a bit of everything! And this was what I decided to do. There was something for everyone and people could come and enjoy themselves. I also chat a lot to the audience at concerts too. I talk about my life, my career, the things I've done, and I always feel at the end of the night that people have got to know me and that they can walk out feeling that they've shared some of my life. All concerts I do are like this and we all have a lot of fun!

I remember three wonderful concerts, in particular, in London. One was a great big charity night at the Royal Festival Hall and everyone, but everyone, was appearing. One of the performers was Vera Lynn who sang her theme song, 'We'll Meet Again', quite beautifully. Later she led us all in the finale, 'Land of Hope and Glory'. It was a little bit too low for me, as it was for the lovely Scottish tenor Kenneth McKellar, who was standing beside me, so we sang it an octave higher. We nearly raised the roof!

Also appearing was Cliff Richard. I had just been on before Cliff and I didn't use the microphone. When Cliff came on stage he said, 'Incredible singers, aren't they, these ones that come on and open their mouth, don't need a microphone, and make themselves heard. Of course, I don't need a microphone either.' With that he moved away from the microphone and just opened his mouth as if he were talking, but didn't let any sound come out! It was a marvellous gag and a delightful send-up of me. I loved it.

Another concert was while I was doing *Robert and Elizabeth* in London. I was asked to do a Sunday afternoon Mozart concert with the Pro Arte Orchestra. I chose a very difficult Mozart concert aria, also 'Dove Sono' from *The Marriage of Figaro* and the Alleluja from *Exsultate, Jubilate*. I hadn't sung anything like this for a long while, having been doing eight performances a week of *Robert and Elizabeth* for the past year, which doesn't leave time for much else. I worked very hard and my arias shaped up well. I heard on the grapevine that people in the music world were coming because they didn't believe I could sing anything like Mozart any more. People were saying things like, 'Oh, we've got to go along. This should be very funny, Bronhill trying to sing those things.'

At one stage I said to my husband, Richard, 'I've got a feeling that I should just opt out of this. They're all coming to laugh at me.'

He said, 'No, you don't opt out. You get up there and do it and show them exactly how well you *can* do it!'

So I did! My first item, the concert aria, brought the house down. It was really terrific and I thought, 'Yes, that's not bad, is it?' In the second half I did 'Dove Sono' for which I got really tremendous applause. Then I sang the Alleluja. The place went absolutely wild. They applauded and applauded – somebody said for ten minutes. I wouldn't know if that's true, but it certainly felt like it to me! I didn't have an encore up my sleeve so I had to sing the Alleluja again. But I think I proved to everyone that I was still a pretty good singer!

Then, on 16 December 1969, the occasion of Noël Coward's seventieth birthday, a midnight concert was arranged to toast the Master. Anyone who had had anything to do with Coward appeared on the programme – and what a galaxy of stars there was! Almost everyone from the theatrical and film worlds was on the stage of the Phoenix Theatre that night. And what a star-studded audience as well! On the stroke of midnight, Coward walked in with the delightful Merle Oberon on his arm. The whole house erupted with cheers and applause for the great man.

When Coward knew that I would be singing, he particularly asked for me to sing Melanie's Aria from *Conversation Piece*, as he thought it was the best piece of music he had written. And it *is* a gem. I don't think I did it justice that night (boy, was I nervous! *And* I didn't sing until 4.30 in the morning!) but I hope that Coward tunes in occasionally from 'up above' and hears me sing it these days. It's a hell of a lot better! What an exciting night that was, and one that none of us who participated will ever forget.

I'll tell you about a few Australian concerts now. The first time I sang in the Sydney Opera House was at a big concert to raise money for Darwin, after it had been almost flattened by Cyclone Tracy. It was a great thrill for me, both to be associated with the cause and to sing in the Opera House. I sang with a wonderful Australian tenor, Donald Smith, who has also sung on many occasions in England. I sang a couple of solos ('Vilja', of course!) and a couple of duets with Smithy. We brought the house down — everybody went wild!

In December 1975 I went back to the Sydney Opera House for two wonderful concerts, the same concert two nights running, called 'An Evening with June Bronhill', with Maestro Tommy Tycho and his orchestra. They were very exciting concerts and great nights. The concert hall was packed out on both occasions and the audiences were lovely; they responded to me warmly. Once again I sang a bit of everything. Tommy Tycho especially arranged a marvellous opening, using the wonderful theme from *2001, A Space Odyssey*. The orchestra was lit in magnificent flashing reds, blues and golds. It was quite electrifying. The music finished in such a way that I could sing my wonderful opening cadenza of *The Daughter of the Regiment* aria off-stage. The effect was dramatic. Then I made my entrance in a wonderful red, floating chiffon dress. It set the seal on a great night in the most spectacular manner.

The audience did some lovely things. For instance, towards the end of the night, when I was doing my encores, my feet were really killing me, and I said, 'My feet are killing me.' One darling man from the back of the auditorium called out, 'Well, take 'em off.'

'What, me feet?' I said.

I always enjoy it when audiences feel that they can talk to me, make comments and yell out things like 'Do so and so, June.' They always call me June, which is lovely.

Both these concerts were recorded and the pick of them put on to a record called 'June Bronhill at the Sydney Opera House'.

A scene from the London production of *The Dancing Years* (1968).

The cover photo of June for the second recording of *The Merry Widow* (1968).

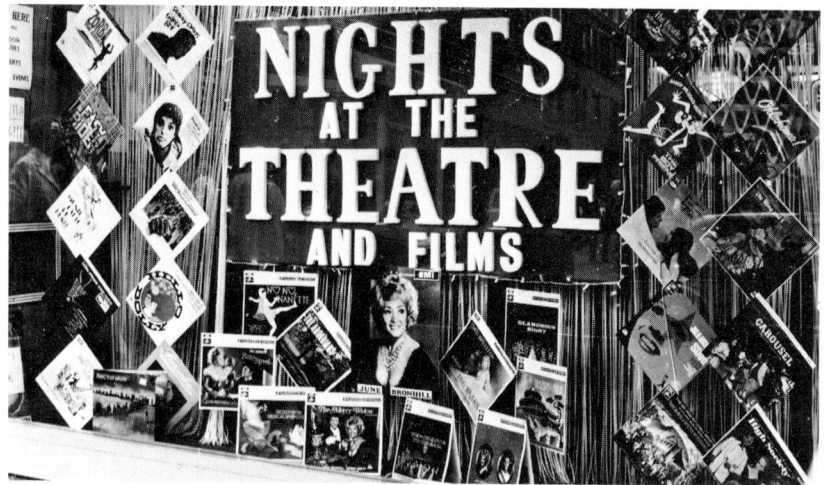

The window of EMI's record store in Oxford Street, London, 1969. June's photo is surrounded by covers of her records.

A scene from Noël Coward's *Bitter Sweet* (1970). June is second from the left.

June with Olive Gilbert in Ivor Novello's musical comedy, *Glamorous Night*.

The Master and star-studded cast on stage at Noël Coward's seventieth birthday concert, held at the Phoenix Theatre in London in December 1969.

June rehearsing with Maestro Tommy Tycho for concerts at the Sydney Opera House, 1975.

A star-studded get-together: (*from top left*) Bob Gibson, June Bronhill, John McNally, Marilyn Rowe, Barry Crocker, John Meehan, Kathryn Selby, James Pegler and Renee Geyer.

In 1977 I did a series of church concerts to raise money for churches on an ecumenical basis. The programme was called 'Songs of Love and Praise'. It went marvellously. They were divine concerts and were well received. I not only sang beautiful songs but also read a lot of poetry. One of the poems that I did was 'Drink to Me Only with Thine Eyes'. At the first rehearsal we had, at St Stephens Church in Macquarie Street, Sydney, I was going through my programme while people were coming in and out of the church to pray or to listen. I was saying that many beautiful poems had been set to music and one such beautiful poem is 'Drink to Me Only'. I was just about to start reading the poem when Werner Baer, who was accompanying me, got into a great state. He said, 'I haven't got the music. You haven't given me the music for this.'

I said, 'If you'd been listening to me, you'd know that I'm not bloody well going to sing it, I'm going to read it.'

The few people in the church looked at me in absolute astonishment and walked out. I felt very ashamed of myself.

At the end of one concert in Bankstown, the minister got up to thank me. He spoke beautifully, saying how wonderful it all was, then he turned to me and said, 'So I must now thank Miss Joan Sutherland for . . .' and he stopped and said, 'I've done it. I said to my wife today, "It's June Bronhill, I must remember that, it's June Bronhill." Now I've done it, I've called you Joan Sutherland.'

I smiled at him and said, 'I have been called much worse.'

I was asked to be part of a big all-Australian concert being arranged by the Australian Government in association with the UNICEF committee in New York, to be held in the General Assembly hall of the United Nations in December 1976. I was absolutely thrilled to be asked and decided that I would sing the marvellous Adam Variations on a Theme by Mozart. We all know this as the tune of 'Twinkle Twinkle Little Star' but it is actually *'Ah, vous dirai-je, maman'*. It is an absolutely incredible concert aria, quite difficult to sing, and I was thrilled when I mastered it.

I had arrived in America and a few nights before the

concert, I had a message to phone Canberra as soon as possible. My immediate thought was, 'They don't want me to sing in the concert because Joan Sutherland is in it as well and I suppose they don't want two sopranos singing!' I was very despondent. I phoned Canberra immediately and was told, 'Miss Bronhill, Her Majesty the Queen would like to know whether you are willing to accept the Order of the British Empire in the New Year's Honours List.' I said, 'Of course I would, I'd be thrilled to.' This was for my services to the performing arts. I was just bowled over – me an OBE! I said, 'That's very exciting.'

'But you mustn't tell anybody. It must be kept a strict secret until it is actually announced in the newspapers.'

'But I'm just so excited and my business manager is sitting here with me and he's going to want to know what's going on. Can I please tell him?'

'Yes, that'll be all right, but nobody else.'

I told Geoffrey Bell, my manager, and he was as thrilled as I was! We toasted JB, OBE then and there.

The concert aria that I was going to perform had a tremendous amount of flute obbligato with voice and they have to work very well together. At my first rehearsal, the flautist was absolutely hopeless and he knew it. He said, 'I'm sorry, but I've never played anything like this before.' I had brought my own conductor, Russell Channell, from the Australia Opera, with me. Russell said, 'I don't know what we're going to do, June, but leave it with me. I'll talk to the powers that be.' The following morning, the day of the concert, we had our rehearsal at the United Nations General Assembly Hall. The organisers said to Russell and me, 'All's well! We have the lead flautist from the Metropolitan Opera.' Well, that was a great joy for me.

The concert was a great success. I think I sang very well and I think they quite liked me in America. But it's the only time I've ever sung there!

Since I've been living back home in Australia, I've done many, many concert tours and, because of the vastness of

Australia, I've really travelled some ground, I can tell you! I have done two concert tours around Victoria; concert tours in the north-east New South Wales; two concert tours in Queensland, which were quite incredible, going right out into the wilds to places like Roma and Mt Isa, both wonderful mining towns, then along the superb Queensland coast to places like Cairns, Townsville and Rockhampton — travelling absolutely miles and doing something like eight concerts in twelve days *plus* all the travelling! But they were wonderful and so exciting to do because a lot of these places don't get as much live entertainment as the bigger cities do. I enjoyed doing these tours tremendously.

I think my favourite concert tour was in May 1981, when I was asked by the Arts Council of Western Australia, in conjunction with the Arts Council of the Northern Territory, to do a tour of the north-west. The tour was also partly sponsored by Mobil Oil and they looked after me incredibly well. I did seventeen concerts in twenty-three days, going to lots of mining towns on the edge of the desert, places like Paraburdoo, Tom Price, Kununurra, Gove, Tennant Creek and Katherine. While the tour was being organised, the Arts Council told me that they had heard from a small gold-mining town right on the edge of the desert in Western Australia called Telfer, saying that they had never had anybody come to entertain them out there. They would outlay all the extra money involved in chartering extra planes and so on if only I could fit Telfer in my itinerary. The Arts Council asked me how I felt about it and I just said of course I'd love to do it.

The population of Telfer is only 300 and there must have been 250 people at the concert that night. They apologised to me afterwards because everybody wasn't there! They said some of the men had to work night shift, of course, and there were a few children in the township who couldn't come! When we left in the morning there must have been a hundred people to wave us all goodbye. I'm so glad we fitted in Telfer.

139

That tour was quite extraordinary. We travelled everywhere by six- or eight-seater planes and flew at about 4000 or 5000 feet across the incredible terrain of the north-west of Western Australia. The landscape was like the paintings of that wonderful artist, Albert Namatjira, with marvellous vibrant greens, blues and ochres. I have never seen such colours or such beauty in my life as I saw while flying over that area.

At Gove the manager of my hotel said, 'Jump in the jeep, June, and I'll show you a lot of the mining districts round here and where a lot of the Aboriginals camp down by the beaches.' So he took me on a wonderful hour's drive showing me these sights. When we got back, just about in time for lunch, his wife rushed out to meet us and said, 'Get June back into the jeep, Alan, because a buffalo is running wild in the town.' Alan explained that there were a few herds of buffalo around the area, but for one of them to stray into the township in the daytime was quite unheard of! We jumped in the jeep and tried to trace the buffalo's tracks. Eventually somebody said it had last been seen heading for the school. We went towards the school and there it was running wild in the playground. The children, of course, were all huddled underneath the school verandahs. They weren't going to be let loose anywhere within cooee of that buffalo. Eventually it ran across the road in front of us and Alan said to me, 'You watch it—you see up there by that fence, that is an old buffalo track, but the buffalo haven't used it for twenty-odd years, but I bet it scents out that old track.' And sure enough it went scooting up this buffalo track and probably found another way across to wherever its herd was. It was a great experience for me to see a buffalo running wild in the town of Gove.

The people from Mobil looked after us wonderfully well. One Sunday in Broome they arranged for us to go deep-sea fishing for lovely great big schnapper. I couldn't catch a thing for love nor money! I was absolutely hopeless, and the others weren't having much luck, either. It was a beautiful warm day, even though it was May. The temperature was probably about 40°C. While I was sitting there, with my line dangling over the side, I started singing 'Summertime' and it all happened! I'd heard that fish love the sound of music, but I certainly didn't think they would react so quickly. I'd just started singing when the fish came right up to the surface of the water. Everybody was pulling them in like there was no tomorrow. They kept saying, 'Don't worry about fishing, June, just sing!' I was the end of a lot of those beautiful fish but they were delicious!

In some of these places, we performed in very ordinary halls, with no air-conditioning, and the heat was very intense, even at night. They had to open doors and windows to try to cool the place down. Of course, the insects came in in droves and they were dive-bombing me! One night, one actually went straight down my throat. I'm happy to say it didn't stop on the way! I took a deep breath and down it went. I didn't even feel it go down, but I saw and felt it go in my mouth. So did the audience, and they absolutely fell about laughing. The insects also dive-bombed down the front of my dress, so I was making passionate gestures with my hand to my breast, hoping I was killing the so-and-sos. Poor David King, my accompanist, had his problems, too. It was so hot that his perspiring hands were sliding off the keys. At times, we couldn't control our laughter and the audience was thoroughly enjoying it as well. One night there was a cockroach crawling across the floor, then it was diving and flying up the walls. It had me in fits of laughter. I stopped singing and said to David, 'What's happening to you over there?'

'My hands are so slippery they just keep falling off the keys, and just come and have a look at my music.'

I had a look. You really couldn't tell what were notes on the music and what was insects!

We finished the tour in Alice Springs, which is one of my favourite places in Australia. We had been to see two beautiful places outside Alice Springs, Simpson's Gap and

Stanley Chasm, where the rock formation is quite incredible and is millions of years old. Seeing all these incredible places with their wonderful quartz outcrops of beautiful colours was so exciting. I said, in passing, that I would have loved to have gone to Ayers Rock. With that, of course, the Mobil boys said, 'Don't worry, June, we've got plenty of time tomorrow before we fly back to Adelaide. We'll arrange it.' They chartered two planes and took us out to Ayers Rock!

★

My first introduction to a proper nightclub was when I was asked to appear in a nightclub called the Lido in Melbourne after I finished *Robert and Elizabeth*. I loved my four weeks there. It was a great introduction to what would later become very much a part of my life – working in the leagues clubs of New South Wales.

These leagues clubs are run either by the Returned Soldiers Leagues or by the football leagues. They make their money out of poker machines. In 1970 I was asked if I would do four weeks at the South Sydney Junior Leagues Club. I just jumped at it. I thought it would be a great thrill to do something new.

I came home to Australia for six weeks and it was great to be back again. In my four-week season I did one show on Thursdays, one on Fridays, and two shows each on Saturdays and Sundays. The auditorium seats over a thousand people, and it was packed to capacity at every performance. They were a lovely audience. You could have heard a pin drop, which I thought was marvellous because I had visions of people drinking and calling for waiters and poker machines making noise.

I had such a great success there that on my closing night the management did something that everyone at the club said they'd never seen them do before – they had a champagne party for me! At the party the club secretary said what a great success it had been and that they hoped I would come back again, to which I said that I'd love to. Then he said, 'You

142

know, it's been such a success that we've made over and above what we normally make on the poker machines – an extra $100,000 just in these few nights that you've been here. We don't even know what we're going to do with it.'

I said, 'Look, I could tell you. I'll help you out of the problem!'

We had a great laugh. They told me that when people enjoy a show, they always go and play the pokies for an hour and hardly anyone ever wins!

South Sydney Junior Leagues Club invited me back the following year for five weeks. When I arrived there on opening night there was a dear old chap, Bill, who worked backstage. Bill said to me, 'Oh, geez, it's good to see ya, June. Ya know, we've 'ad that Kathleen Greystones here [he meant Kathryn Grayson] and we've had so many big names, but it's always lovely to have you back because you're Australian – you're one of us.'

I said, 'Well, Bill, it's lovely to be back. I loved this club last year and I'm sure I'm going to enjoy it this year.'

'But look, June, now look, while I've got you standin' 'ere talkin' to me, I was wonderin' whether or not you'd settle a bet I've 'ad with a mate of mine.'

'Well, if I can Bill, of course I will.'

'Now look, 'e said to me that your name was Joan and I said, no it's not, it's June.'

'Well, you've won the bet, Bill. My name is June.'

'That's what I said to him – June Brommell.'

That year I also did a week at Granville RSL Club, which was marvellous. Club work was wonderful for me because I found that I was reaching yet another audience – and I never sang down to them. A lot of people said, 'Oh, you can't sing any opera at the clubs,' but I said, 'We'll see! I think I can.' This was particularly borne out when I next came back to Australia in 1973. I did six clubs in six weeks, once again working one show on Thursday and Fridays and two shows on Saturdays and Sundays.

I brought Brian Stanborough with me to be my

accompanist. He is a fellow Australian with whom I'd worked a lot in London. When we left London we still hadn't worked out a proper programme! Suddenly the idea hit me of putting my life story to music and singing the songs associated with it, starting with the first song I ever sang. We'd see how much of it I could get into the hour and a half expected of me. Brian liked my idea. So over lunch at Doyles, a marvellous fish restaurant in Sydney, we worked out my programme on a table napkin. We timed it so that I would stop at 1961 when I came back to Australia to do *The Sound of Music*, because I also wanted to talk about my recording career and my home life in Broken Hill, singing some of the lovely songs of yesteryear.

The first club was North Sydney Leagues Club. When I arrived there to rehearse, the first person I saw was darling David Gray with whom I'd worked many times before, in *Orpheus in the Underworld* and *The Merry Widow*. He had also sung with me at South Sydney Junior Leagues Club in 1970 and 1971. David asked me what duets we were doing. I said, 'We're not, love. I'm doing something quite different this time. I'm not using the orchestra because they didn't give me time to get orchestrations done, so I brought Brian Stanborough with me.'

The club secretary found us a room with a piano, and Brian and I started rehearsing. The first thing I sang was the *Daughter of the Regiment* aria. Then the secretary said, 'Oh, you're not going to sing that opera stuff, are you?'

'I am, actually.'

'Oh, you can't sing that sort of stuff to club audiences.'

'I know exactly what club audiences like. I have my programme organised and that is that.'

'You can't sing things like that. You've got to give them ordinary stuff.'

'I will not be told what I must sing, and what I must not sing. I will not sing down to my audience. I will give them my best.'

'Well, I'm afraid it's not right for here.'

144

'Now, I will tell you one thing, if you are not out of this room by the time I count to five, you won't even have me on your programme tonight. I will just walk out and it will be your fault.'

He said, 'Oh, well . . .' and I said, 'One . . . two . . . three . . .' and with that he went!

I went on stage that night and it was a wow. I did two hours non-stop and members of the audience became quite involved. When I was talking about the break-up of my first marriage I was saying things like, 'If things aren't working in a marriage, there's no point in hanging on, is there?' and women were coming to me and saying, 'I quite agree, love.' They wanted to tell me their troubles. It was just a wild success, with a standing ovation at the end.

That club season really was fantastic. Everywhere we went we did at least two hours, generally two and a quarter hours, and that without an interval! And the audiences didn't want to go. They all said, 'We want to hear what happens after 1961.' Eveywhere it was standing ovations and audience participation. I just absolutely love doing these clubs! I've been doing clubs all these years that I've been living in Australia again, performing all over New South Wales. When people say to me, 'How can you bear to work in the clubs? Isn't the noise terrible?' I say, 'No, it isn't. You can literally hear a pin drop.' I think it's because I'm singing the songs that people want to hear and I talk to them and tell them jokes and we laugh and we cry and it's a great night's fun and a great night's entertainment – even if I do say so myself!

★

My introduction to variety came before I had auditioned for Sadler's Wells or sung anywhere. I was asked to appear in Bradford at the Alhambra Theatre for a week of variety concerts given by the Bradford police. They had the police choir and the police band on the programme. What a week that was! Bradford, in Yorkshire, is the centre of the cotton mill industry, and this was in November. It rained all the time and there was thick heavy smog. The police were outrageous. I've never seen so much booze put away in my life as they did that week!

At about the same time, another of Dino Borgioli's students was organising a variety show for charity at the old Casino Theatre in London's West End and asked me to take part. It was a great night and the theatre was packed. The little unknown soprano, June Bronhill, received a rousing reception. There were lots of famous people on the bill and a few I hadn't heard of as well! This concert took place when the song 'I Believe' first appeared on the scene. Something must have gone wrong with the organisation because no less than three people sang 'I Believe' at that concert. About halfway through the second half, Benny Hill came on and brought the house down by saying, 'I would like to sing a new song that I'm sure many of you haven't heard before, "I Believe".'

Harry Secombe had a bad cold that night but, rather than let everyone down, he went on and sang—quite magnificently. The audience went wild but Harry just couldn't cope with singing again. He went back on and took a curtain call, then went offstage. Still the audience stamped and cheered. Standing in the wings was Spike Milligan. He was not appearing in the concert; he was just keeping Harry company. When the applause wouldn't stop, Spike went on stage and did Harry's encore. It was just so funny and the audience went even wilder!

Over the years I became involved in a lot of variety shows held on Sunday nights during summer at the Opera House in Blackpool. These shows always had top stars heading the bill, people like Max Bygraves, Harry Secombe and Russ Conway. I was often asked to be second billing. The Opera House at Blackpool seats probably as many as 3,000 people and they were always hanging from the rafters. We did two shows, one at six o'clock and one at 8.30, and you couldn't get a seat for love nor money. They were great shows, with great entertainers and I was honoured to be part of them. They also prepared me for the big one – the London Palladium.

When I was offered second billing to Tommy Steele at the London Palladium I was absolutely bowled over. Me, performing at the London Palladium, perhaps the top variety theatre in the world! We had the most incredible out-of-town try-out – three weeks in Toronto at the O'Keefe Centre!

I've also been involved with a number of Royal Command Variety Performances over the years. My first was when I was doing *The Merry Widow* at the London Coliseum. That year the Royal Command Performance was held at the Coliseum and the finale of the show consisted of the three main shows on in the West End at the time, the ones that were really packing them in. There was Sadler's Wells' *The Merry Widow*; there was *My Fair Lady* with Julie Andrews and Rex Harrison; and there was *Charlie's Aunt* with Norman Wisdom. I wasn't presented to the Queen because there was such a tremendous line-up of performers, but I didn't mind really because I did get a lovely certificate, signed by the Queen, to say that I had appeared!

I sang at a lovely royal concert at the London Palladium before the Queen Mother and was presented to her afterwards. She was quite the most charming woman, and she had time to talk to us all, commenting on our work. Then, the time I was doing *The Dancing Years*, I was asked to appear in a wonderful Command Performance at Drury Lane. I wore my beautiful costume from the Belvedere Garden scene, which was actually a Regency gown, about 120 years old. It was made of what had once been black velvet but with age had turned a lovely brownish black, and was trimmed with gorgeous lace. Prince Philip and Princess Anne attended that performance.

When I made my entrance I acknowledged the royal box and I was highly delighted to see Prince Philip lean forward, fold his arms on the edge of the box and look at me quite interestedly. When we were presented afterwards, Prince

147

Philip talked to me about my singing and my work, then he came back to me a couple of times later to chat about Broken Hill. I said to the person next me (I believe it was Judi Dench), 'I've got a feeling I might be the next royal mistress!' It never happened, though!

In Australia, I have sung at two Royal Command Performances, both of them before Prince Charles. At the time of the first one, I was doing a show which was about the lovely music of Sigmund Romberg. At the Command Performance, I appeared with my group of singers and we did a selection from our show. When I was presented to Prince Charles he said, 'I've heard a lot about you from my family.' I was floored! Then he looked behind me and said, 'And this is your extended barbershop quartet, I presume.' We had a lovely chat.

Then in 1981, not long after his engagement to Lady Diana was announced, I was asked to sing at a Royal Command Performance in Adelaide. I was just about to fly to England for the new production of *The Sound of Music* so I sang some songs from the show. First I sang 'Edelweiss'. When I finished I said, 'I didn't really want to sing that song at all. I wanted to sing a lovely comedy song by Noël Coward called "Chase Me Charlie", but they told me I was a bit too late!' The audience and Prince Charles had a good laugh, and when I was presented to Prince Charles afterwards, he said, 'Tell me truthfully, June, did Noël Coward really write a song called "Chase Me Charlie"?' I said yes and to prove it, I sang a couple of bars of the song for him.

★

I was rather thrilled when the State Theatre Company of South Australia asked me if I would do a play for them. It was Joan Littlewood's wonderful show, *Oh, What a Lovely War*, but we were doing an Australian version, *Oh, What a Lovely War, Mate!*. It was a wonderful company and a wonderful cast. I acted a few parts and sang some great songs.

148

One of them was that marvellous 'On Sunday I Go Out with a Soldier', which was great fun. I wore a fabulous costume, a Mae-West-looking thing. I also sang 'Keep the Home Fires Burning' which was a moving moment in the show. It was all something new for me. While it wasn't really a straight play, I was still working with a professional theatre company for the first time in my life.

As a result of that the company asked me to do a play for them, *The Last Day at Woolloomooloo* by Ron Blair. The play takes place in this old boarding-house in Woolloomooloo, a wharfside area in Sydney. I was to play the landlady, rough as guts but with a heart of gold, a real down-to-earth Aussie woman. It was a wonderful play and another new experience for me. Luckily, for my first venture in straight theatre, I had a marvellous director, Colin George, who was also the director of the theatre company. Colin was a great help to me, and I learned a lot.

Some years later I was asked to do an American play, a comedy called *Women Behind Bars*. My part was the matron of a prison, who was a nasty evil lesbian. When I read the script I couldn't believe it. It was funny, but very black and blue. At first I couldn't see me doing it, but then I met the producers and read for them. They wanted me to read the two most bawdy parts of the whole play. The language was unreal, but I thought, 'Oh, well, nothing ventured, nothing gained.' And I really got into it! They loved it; they fell about laughing and said it was marvellous. So it was decided then and there that I would play Pauline (whom everybody calls Paul!), the matron.

The play was a marvellous spoof on all those women's prison movies of the 1940s and 1950s. It very much resembled the classic, *Caged*. We had a wonderful cast of ten women and one man, and what fun we had! But it was actually hard work for all of us. Of course, a lot of my fans were shattered when they heard that I was going to do something so naughty, but I assured them that it wouldn't change me as a person!

One day the house manager said to me at the end of the performance, 'June, I have to tell you this. We had a party in today of forty-five middle-aged ladies who were in Sydney for a bowling convention. They'd seen June Bronhill was on and came especially to see you.'

'Did they leave?' I asked.

'Oh, no. They sat there and they laughed all the way through. They seemed to enjoy it.'

It was a wonderful challenge for me to do that play. I think the reason my career has diversified so much is that I love a challenge. One of the most important things for any performer is to have a challenge. I could have had quite a career as an opera singer and I would have had many challenges in an operatic career, but I might have been bored doing the same style of thing all the time, and I've never been bored once in the whole of my career. It is the challenge of plays like *Women Behind Bars* that I find so stimulating and I welcome that challenge, head on!

Recently I did a wonderful show, *Songs from Sideshow Alley*, written by Robyn Archer, an excellent playwright and entertainer. The show is about two old dears, Trixie and Pearl, who run stalls in the alleys of shows, like the Royal Easter Show, that go all around the countryside. They've been together for about forty years and they absolutely adore each other. It was a really great show with these two old girls and a couple of musicians joining in. It's a one-acter, about one and a half hours long, and you don't stop! It was exhausting but very fulfilling.

The role I played, Trixie, was a marvellous character with a heart of gold and ever hopeful about the future of the alley. I looked hysterical, wearing baggy old trousers, braces, a funny old shirt, a 'wide boy' necktie, a jacket that was part of the uniform of the sideshow alley people, and a battered old panama hat. At the end of one performance I was told about a dear old lady who went up to one of the ushers and asked, 'Excuse me, when's June Bronhill coming on?' Didn't recognise me!

During the run of the show it was amazing the number of people I didn't know who came up to see me afterwards and said, 'We were just waiting for you to sing "Vilja" from *The Merry Widow.*'

We did an amazing tour around South Australia and the Northern Territory. Most of the time we travelled by car or bus. We did something like twenty-seven towns in seven weeks, and that's hard work, I can tell you! Particularly in the heart of South Australia and up in the Northern Territory when you play in places like Coober Pedy, Woomera and Gove where the temperature can be 40°C or 45°C!

*

Over the years I have recorded something like thirty LPs of operetta, musical comedy, sacred songs and all sorts of lovely things that, I'm happy to say, people have enjoyed buying. Most of my recordings have been done for EMI and I became popular there. I got to know the whole recording staff well.

The first recording I ever made was the Sadler's Wells production of *The Merry Widow.* On our first day of recording, towards the end of our three-hour session, Norman Newell of EMI said to me, 'June, would you mind if we just do a sound check for "Vilja"?' Naturally, I agreed. 'We won't have time to record it, but we'll have it ready to go first up tomorrow,' he said. So they checked everything as I sang it through. At the end everyone in the control room said, 'That's it.'

'OK. See you tomorrow,' I said.

'No, that's it.'

'What do you mean, that's it?'

'It's in the can.'

'It was OK?'

'It was perfect. The sound was absolutely perfect, everything was marvellous, so it's down.'

So I became known at EMI after that as 'One-take

Bronhill'! It didn't always happen that way, though!

The recording of the Sadler's Wells *Merry Widow* was the first time the payment of royalties to the cast was handled by British Actors Equity under a new system. Each performer was given so many points according to the size of the role performed and paid accordingly. That *Merry Widow* recording sold like hot cakes. My first royalty cheque was about £250 for three months' sales—at threepence a record!—and even today, nearly thirty years later, I still get regular cheques from Equity. That lovely *Widow* is still selling well. It was the first of a series of recordings of Wells productions done with EMI and I'm still getting royalties for all of them!

A few years later I recorded *The Arcadians* for EMI. I worked on the score with Anthony Kinsella, a New Zealander who was a brilliant concert pianist and who also gave master classes to instrumentalists and singers. When it came to studying the song, 'The Pipes of Pan', he said to me, 'June, sing it quite differently from the majority of coloratura sopranos. Make the pipes sound like pipes. Take it very fast, so that it really has a wonderful pipey sound.' I loved doing it this way, because when I had last sung it, umpteen years before, I had sung it the usual way, making a meal of it. Tossing it off was such fun!

At the recording session, I said to Vilem Tausky, our conductor, a wonderful man I'd worked with many times before, 'Mr Tausky, I must tell you that, with regard to "The Pipes of Pan", I do it very quickly.'

He replied, 'You sing it, June, and I will follow you.'

So we started rehearsing and I took it like the wind! Tausky said, 'Oh, no, June, it's much too fast.' Everybody agreed with him.

I said, 'I don't care what any of you say, I want to sing it that way—I want it to be quite different.'

So we rehearsed it again, very fast. It really went like the pipes of Pan! Afterwards they all agreed with me that it was all right, to which I replied that it was just as well, because that was how I was going to sing it. I really had a bee in my bonnet!

At the end of the recording session, a quite elderly violinist from the orchestra said to me, 'June, I was in the orchestra for the original production in London of *The Arcadians*.'

I thought, 'Oh, dear, he's going to say something about my "Pipes of Pan".'

He went on, 'And I must tell you, this is the first time I've heard "The Pipes of Pan" sung as it was originally — nice and quickly, fast and like pipes. I was pleased that you stood up for yourself.'

Good on you, Anthony Kinsella!

One thing I hate doing is putting my voice down over a pre-recorded orchestral track. It's done all the time now, but I miss the personal contact with the musicians and conductors. I don't think there's anything quite like that atmosphere of the voices, the orchestra and the conductor working together at the same time, in the same place.

When I made a recording with David Gray called *Together*, in which we sang lots of lovely duets from various musicals, plus a couple of solos each, I had been out of Sydney, so Tommy Tycho and his orchestra, with David, had put down the soundtracks for all the duets. When I came back to Sydney, I put down the voice-over with David. No singer ever sings anything exactly the same way twice. In this case, all the tempi were put down the way Tommy and David felt them, not being able to consult me. Consequently, I found a lot of the recorded tempi slow, which is a shame because it could have been a great recording and sold a lot more copies. It didn't have the impact it should have had, although a lot of people do like it very much.

The converse is that some years later I put down a marvellous recording with Dennis Olsen and the Adelaide ABC Orchestra. We recorded the show we did called *Together with Music* which was based on Ivor Novello and Noël Coward. The conductor was marvellous Gerald Krug. We were all together in the recording studio and it was absolutely lovely, a joy to record. I much prefer working this way.

★

After the success of *The Merry Widow*, the BBC started using me quite regularly in all sorts of programmes, mainly in the Light Music Department, shows like 'Friday Night is Music Night', 'Variety Playhouse', 'Max Jaffa's Palm Court Orchestra'—shows with lovely light music and the odd operatic aria thrown in. I broadcast on the BBC so regularly that all my friends started calling it the Bronhill Broadcasting Corporation!

In the early 1970s I was associated with some lovely tributes broadcast by the BBC from Festival Hall. Once was a tribute to Noël Coward and the other was a tribute to Ivor Novello. I've always been a great admirer of both these composers. I was also very honoured and excited when the BBC did a series called 'Leading Ladies'. I was one of their leading ladies and people paid tribute to me!

★

I've done a lot of television, both in England and in Australia. I adore the medium, I suppose because I'm one of those people who always reacts to a camera. Whenever a camera appears on the scene, I smile. I kind of 'switch on'!

When I came back to Australia in 1975 to sing Gilda in *Rigoletto* for the Australian Opera Company, my business manager, Geoffrey Bell, had arranged a lovely press reception at his apartment. When one of the television interviews went to air, they'd got everything back to front, because apart from doing Gilda in Australia, I was also going to New Zealand to do *The Merry Widow*. They'd got it the other way round! Some time later Geoffrey asked me to keep a particular date free as that television channel wanted to re-interview me to make up for the mix-up they had made originally.

Eventually the day arrived. I didn't want to do this TV thing at all. I was busy rehearsing *Rigoletto* and thought the whole thing was pointless, as it was months since they'd made the mistake. I had to have my hair done and went to my hairdresser in David Jones. I started phoning for a taxi about five o'clock, when my hair was nearly finished but I couldn't get one (it was Friday). Then I tried to ring Geoffrey at his office (I was supposed to go from his place to the studios) but he had left. I tried to reach him at home but he wasn't there. Time was passing and I still couldn't get a taxi. Eventually I got Geoffrey at home and said, 'Will you bring the blue dress I decided to wear on this wretched thing? And I still think you're out of your mind.' I was in a foul temper and said, 'What time do you think you'll get here?'

Geoffrey said, 'They're sending a car to take us out to the studios, so we'll meet you outside David Jones.'

'What sort of car?'

'A white Rolls Royce.'

I thought, 'Well, they're really going mad, aren't they?'

Eventually Warren, my hairdresser, and I went downstairs—to find the store closed! We couldn't get out of the building. So I did a quick, loud cooee up the lift shaft and after about twenty minutes the night watchman came down and let us out. By this time it was about half past six. I was standing outside the store, in the rain, waiting for the car, and I was really in a rotten mood.

After a while the white Rolls arrived. Geoffrey tried to calm me down and was being charming, but I kept saying, 'I'm not interested. The whole thing is ludicrous.'

At Channel 7 there was a crowd on the doorstep, waiting for me. They were all in a panic. I said I was sorry I was so late and told them the story about getting locked in David Jones. Everyone was charming. They took me away, put me in a little room on my own and found me a scotch. I was up to my ears in temper. After I'd been there about half an hour they took me in to make-up. Everyone was making sure I couldn't hear what was going on. They brought the interviewer in to make sure he had everything right this time. I had a tickly cough and I was chewing a throat sweet.

At last I was taken in for the interview. I looked around. It was a very elegant setting – chaise-longue, chairs, grand piano and a pedestal with a beautiful floral arrangement. I thought, 'They're really going over the top for this one.' I saw some festooned curtains and thought, 'That's strange. What are they doing there?' As I was walking, still chewing on the cough sweet, the person I thought was going to interview me said, 'Miss Bronhill, do you know Mike Willesee?'

'I've heard of him but never met him. How do you do, Mike?'

With that, the curtains went up, revealing a great audience, and he said, 'June Bronhill, this is your life.'

I said, still chewing, 'You've got to be joking. We don't have it in Australia.'

'We have since last week but it hasn't gone to air yet. You are our second. The first one was Sir Robert Helpmann.'

I couldn't believe it. Then people I had been rehearsing with at the Sydney Opera House appeared, to talk about my life. They hadn't let on; they didn't even know that each other was going on! It was hysterical!

Even to this day I can't believe that it all happened after I'd been locked in David Jones!

I appeared on one of Ronnie Corbett's shows when he did a TV series in Australia. It was tremendous fun. We sent each other up because we're both knee-high to grasshoppers! We did a marvellous spoof on *Traviata*. It was really very funny.

As a result of that performance I was asked to play the corresponding role of Mrs Slocum in the Australian production of *Are You Being Served?*. I was absolutely thrilled that they wanted me. I think I was destined to play that role, actually! Some years before, I did a big charity concert at a grammar school in Sydney. During the show the headmaster's wife said to my friend Freddie, 'I hope you don't think I'm rude, but isn't June like Mrs Slocum?'

When they told me that John Inman was coming out from England to do his role of Mr Humphreys, well, that was it, and I jumped at it! So I became Mrs Crawford who was very much like Mrs Slocum. I think they must have been relatives! We had similar bouffant hairstyles, sometimes blue, sometimes pink, and sometimes talked terribly posh and other times with our own natural accent. We did sixteen episodes altogether. They were a tremendous success. Everybody just loved it, including me. We had great fun. John Inman was wonderful to work with, so helpful and kind.

There was a marvellous episode in which Mrs Crawford had to take charge of our floor. I sat up in the big office and was thrilled about it all to start with. But eventually I became very bored and missed being down on the floor with the others. Mr Humphreys came up to discuss a few things while I was having tea, so I poured him a cup and offered him the lamingtons. Suddenly an enormous blow-fly zoomed down at the lamington I was eating. I brushed it away but it attacked again. This went on for about ten minutes. The audience was in stitches, and John and I could no longer control ourselves. Then everyone was chasing this wretched blowie all over the studio trying to kill it. Eventually we did get it and found a fresh lamington, and we started the scene all over again.

We were all very sorry when the series was over, and unfortunately we haven't been able to do any more because it is so difficult getting everybody together at the same time. It is now about seven years since we did them and they are still being replayed regularly all over Australia.

I've also done a couple of television commercials. I did one for Kambrook, one for Cornelius Furs and one for Liptons tea. In the Liptons ad I hammed it up as a very snooty Toorak lady who has obviously never set foot in a supermarket in her life. I finished it singing a very high note, which was quite a giggle. After that lots of people came up to me in the street and said, 'I saw you in the tea ad.' Even little kiddies said, 'You're the teapot lady, aren't you?' I loved that; I thought it was great.

I have done one thing which has not yet gone to air, but I think it will be screened by the time this book comes out. It is a mini series about Dame Nellie Melba, our first Australian diva. I have a lovely cameo role in the first episode. I play a woman who runs a touring opera company which performs in Mackay, in Queensland, where Nellie lived after she married Charles Armstrong. Nellie went to see the opera and was absolutely thrilled by it. Annis Montague, the character I played, listened to Nellie sing and advised her to follow an operatic career. This gem of a role was lovely to do. Parts were shot on location in Queensland. To me, it was like filming a real movie, and I thought it was a great experience.

★

Well, there we are. Variety *is* the spice of live. It certainly has been with me. But one thing I haven't done is a movie. I would love to do a cameo role in a film – I'd love a bigger role, too! I hope that some day, in the not-too-distant future, you'll see me up there on the big silver screen!

12

Me, Men and Marriage

Where do I begin? I can assure you that the statement I heard at one of my early rehearsals at Sadler's Wells is not true – all coloratura sopranos are *not* nymphomaniacs! I must admit I love men, I adore them – I'd much rather have friendships with fellows than with females – but I haven't really had a promiscuous love life. I'll tell you about some of the special ones.

When I was twenty and living with Barbara and Sam, I was working in a store in Bankstown called Hacketts. One day when I was behind my counter in the manchester department, up to my ears in sheets and towels, a nice-looking man came in and asked if I could tell him where the corsetry department was. I directed him to it. All the girls rather flipped and thought he was something else – I agreed. Then a few weeks later I was contacted by the Petersham Musical Society to see if I would play Margot in *The Desert Song* for them. I said, 'Yes, I've never done anything like it before. Why have you asked me?' They said, 'The man who is directing it is called Brian Martin. He has seen you in the Sun Aria semi-finals and he won't direct it for us unless you play Margot.' So I agreed. They told me when the first rehearsal was and when I arrived who should the director be but the man I'd directed to the corset department! He worked for Berlei. I did a double take and said, 'You're the one that wants me.' He said, 'Oh yes, I do.' He drove me home that night and from there on our romance started. He was a smoothie if ever there was one and I was quite bowled over. He was very clever and intelligent, and we talked music a lot. He had directed a number of productions for Sydney's leading amateur company, the Sydney Opera Society.

On the opening night of *The Desert Song* Brian said he'd collect me and drive me to the Petersham Town Hall where we were performing. On the way the car broke down. By the time the NRMA fixed it we were running late, so I started to put my make-up on in the car. We arrived about ten minutes before curtain up and I was shaking like a leaf— as well as the usual nerves I was extra-nervous because I was late. Everybody was outside the hall waiting for me, all panicking. When we arrived the president of the society was standing there with a glass of scotch. He said to me, 'Here, drink this on your way in before you get dressed. It will calm you down.' I had never had anything hard to drink in my life. It was a pretty nifty neat scotch, so when I downed it, it nearly knocked me for a loop! Fifteen minutes later, when I made my first appearance in the musical, I fell flat on my face—I tripped, I assure you! I decided I wouldn't have neat scotch again for a long, long while. And I didn't!

Soon after this, I left Barbara and Sam's place in Bankstown and found myself a room in a nice flat on the North Shore. Because I was swanning around everywhere with Brian, I hadn't really been in touch with my family. They were worried about me. I hadn't even told Barbara where I was staying. Eventually, they found me because Barbara heard that I was now working at the NRMA. She told me that Dad was very upset and was on his way over from Robe to see me. Dad asked me about Brian and I explained who he was and how we'd met. I said, 'I'm going out with him tonight. He's coming to collect me here at Barbara's.' Dad asked what Brian did and I said he worked for Berlei's.

'Oh, I see—he's a corset peddler.'

He said he didn't want me to go out with Brian and asked me how old he was. I said that Brian was eleven years older than me. My father rather thought Brian could see I had a good career ahead of me and he was going to try to cash in on it. I couldn't see this at all. Dad said, 'Make up your mind – if you go out with him tonight I won't be at all happy. But it's your bed, you've made it, you have to lie on it.'

Of course I went out with Brian. I had made my bed and, my God, I did lie on it, in no uncertain manner, because as time went on things weren't as wonderful as I thought they would be. When it came to us marrying, though, me being a Catholic and Brian being a divorced Catholic, it meant we couldn't get married in a Catholic church, because in the eyes of the Catholic Church, Brian was still married. So we got married in a registry office. We were due to be married one afternoon in August 1951 at 4.30, but we were miles behind with our arrangements and we just couldn't possibly get to the registry office by that time. So Brian got in touch with them and asked if we could make it a bit later. We were eventually married at six o'clock. Many years later someone said to me, 'I don't know whether that's legal, because you were married out of office hours, and if the registry office is legally meant to be closed, I wonder if you were ever legally married to Brian.' I'd love to know!

To start with, we were very happy. But Brian was not a very thoughtful lover, and I didn't know any of the great joys of making love. I was still swept off my feet by him, though, and would pretend I was satisfied. We found a flat next-door to his parents, which was about the worst thing we could have ever done. Then I really got to know Mrs Martin (I couldn't call Mum or Mother). She would come in every morning and say, 'I've come to clean Brian's shoes. Have you put out his clean shirt? Have you done this and that?'

I'd say, 'Yes.'

She'd say, 'Oh, I do all of that sort of thing for him every morning. If you won't do them, he won't change.'

I said, 'I can clean his shoes.'

So I set about doing all these things for him – clean shoes, clean shirt laid out on the bed, clean underwear, socks turned just the right way so he could just slip his feet into them, pressed his suit every morning, and so on. Also, I'd never really cooked in my life and I was tackling things for the first time. Mrs Martin was always there telling me what to do and what not to do, and I did become depressed by all of this. I was twenty-two and I wanted to be left alone to find my own way to set up house and home.

One night when Brian sat down to dinner, I had cooked quite a nice meal except for the peas, which were like bullets. I discovered that night if you overcook peas they go even harder. I put them down in front of Brian and apologised. He said one of the nicest things he could have said, 'That's all right, love, I like my peas like this.'

After about six months we went to England so that I could study. Brian got a job again with Berlei's. Within a year or so I started feeling not very happy. I suppose sexually I was unhappy, and Brian loved going out and playing cricket with 'the boys'. I would go as well but afterwards it would be off to the pub, boozing. I didn't drink at all and I found it rather boring so I stopped going to cricket. He wouldn't come home until about 11.30 or 12 at night. I would be very upset and worried by then. I used to ask him why he'd been out late but he wouldn't even answer me, let alone argue with me. He'd just climb into bed and say nothing. If only we had argued a few times, we could have cleared the air a bit and things would have been a lot happier.

When we had been married about five years Brian had a nervous breakdown. This happened while I was rehearsing for the role of the Queen of Night in *The Magic Flute* for Sadler's Wells. He had told me some three or four months earlier that he would have a nervous breakdown within six months. Of course I thought it was just a joke but, blow me down, he *did* have one. He had to be rushed to hospital, the French Hospital in Shaftesbury Avenue.

The medical staff said they couldn't work out why he had had the breakdown. He didn't seem to be living under any stress, but it had definitely happened and he would have to have shock treatment. Brian wanted me to be at the

162

hospital in the mornings before he went into the shock treatment and come back at lunch time when he would be coming out of it. I was rehearsing hard for *The Magic Flute*. I would call into the hospital about half past eight or nine every morning on my way to Sadler's Wells. Luckily it was on the way; I passed the hospital every morning in the bus. I would see Brian and try to calm him. Then after he had gone to his treatment, I would jump on the bus and go to Sadler's Wells. I'd rehearse until one, grab a sandwich and eat it on the bus on the way to the hospital and sit with him while he came out of the treatment. Then I'd hop on the bus and go back to Sadler's Wells again, rehearse in the afternoon, finish at five, be down at the hospital again by 5.30 and sit with Brian until lights-out at eight. Then I'd get on the bus and go home to Barnes, where we lived, cook myself some dinner and absolutely collapse. After about three months, Brian was able to go back to work at Berlei.

I don't think he realised how unhappy I was, as I persevered with the marriage. For two years I was reasonably happy, then for seven years I was really quite miserable. I was working hard with Sadler's Wells and I'd done *The Merry Widow* towards the end of this period. I'd also become very busy with the BBC. I was asked to do a tremendous amount of broadcasting and lots of concerts, because the *Widow* really started me on a new career away from Sadler's Wells. With all my broadcasting, various concerts and money from Sadler's Wells, I was earning £70 to £100 a week, which was quite a lot of money in those days.

One day, when I came home from a tour with Sadler's Wells, Brian said, 'I've decided to give in my notice at Berlei's. I don't want to work there any more.'

'What are you going to do?'

'I haven't made up my mind.'

'I'm earning quite good money, so take your time. Take three months off and work out exactly what you want to do.'

Three months turned into six months and then a year. When we came to Australia to do *The Merry Widow*, naturally Brian came with me. He became friendly with a few press people whom he had met at some of our press receptions. They were great guys, but they liked to gather at the pub mid-afternoon and of course Brian joined them. Consequently, nearly every time I saw him, he was tiddly. After a few weeks, I couldn't bear it any longer. I was at the stage where I felt repulsed if he touched me. I thought, 'I can't endure this any longer.' One night in bed, when he asked me what was wrong, I said, 'Brian, I have to be honest, I do not love you any more and I want to get a divorce.' Poor love, he was in a terrible state. He broke down crying and said he couldn't exist without me, and if I did that he would kill himself. I had to pull myself together and be strong. I said, 'Brian, frankly, it takes tremendous courage to kill yourself and I don't think you've got the courage to do it. You have to get away, and not depend on me. You rely on me for nearly everything. I have to do everything, even paying the bills, which you never think of. You can't even pack a suitcase – I have to pack and unpack, hang everything up, and do the lot. It's taking too much out of me. My career is getting very busy now and I can't keep this up any longer. You haven't got the courage to kill yourself, but you must find the courage from somewhere to make a life for yourself without me.' And that was that.

I think one of the hardest things of that break-up was having to make Brian pack his own suitcases. I couldn't pack them for him now. I had to watch him and suggest things when he was having difficulties. It was dreadful. Luckily Brian's sister and her family lived in Melbourne, so he went to live with them for a while. Some months later we were divorced.

By his first marriage, Brian had a daugher called Faith, who was nine years younger than me. She came to live with us when we were in London and we were more or less like sisters, a young sister and an older sister. When Brian and I broke up I wrote to Faith in London and told her that her father and I were going to get a divorce. It was for her to decide whether she wanted to move out and live by herself in London or come back to Australia and live with Brian, or stay with me. I had a lovely letter from her saying she wasn't in the least surprised, she was just amazed I had put up with things for as long as I had and that she'd love to stay in London with me. So we became even dearer friends than ever and, while I don't see her very much these days, we still have a deep affection for one another.

Brian, I am happy to say, married again to a lovely woman, Betty, who loved him dearly as he loved her. She made him a wonderful wife – far better than I ever could – until he died a few years ago.

In 1961 Faith and I went on a summer holiday together to Italy, to a place called Noli on the Riviera dei Fiori. One day we were sitting at a table under an umbrella having our drinks before lunch when Faith suddenly said, 'Here comes a very dishy man.' I looked over my sunglasses as he walked past us and I thought, 'Mm, he is nice!' Very well dressed in a grey suit, white shirt, subdued tie. Very handsome, tall and dark. I said to Faith, 'You watch it. He'll be after you.' Then he came back and I said, 'Here he comes, Faith.' When he stopped, he spoke to me! I didn't speak much Italian – I understood a few words. I explained to him that I didn't understand Italian, I was English. He sat down and we had a funny conversation in sign language. Eventually he said he'd like to take me to dinner that night. I found out that his name was Ivano Giustini and I told him where we were staying. They had a beautiful restaurant at the hotel and he said he'd take me there for dinner. After he'd gone, Faith and I shrieked with laughter that it was me that he fancied. That night we had a lovely meal and danced – it really was quite romantic! Ivano came to see me every day. He explained that he was a representative for ICI and that after he finished in this area he had to go Alassio, San Remo and other places on the Riviera. He asked if I had to go straight back to London and as I still had another two weeks before I was due back to Sadler's Wells, I thought I'd stay on an extra week. When I told Faith, she said, 'I don't blame you—half your luck!'

So I had a magical week with Ivano. We made wonderful love, ate wonderfully, laughed ourselves silly. He was a typical mad Italian when you got to know him. His favourite music was Frank Sinatra singing 'All the Way' which he sang, no matter where we went, and it really was hilarious. People say all Italians can sing, the way they say all Welsh people can sing. I can tell you it isn't true. Ivano could not sing! At the end of the week I had to go back, but we planned that I would come back for a week before I was due to to go Australia to do *The Sound of Music*.

We wrote terrific letters to each other. I'd found a marvellous set of recordings called 'Instant Italian' and you also got a dictionary and a wonderful book. I would sit for hours composing my letters to Ivano which were pretty good—he said I was doing very well—warm, loving and funny, and we had a lot of fun with our correspondence.

Before packing to go to Australia I met Ivano in Milan. We drove to Como for a lovely week swimming, loving, eating, drinking—having the most wonderful time. I think I was madly in love with him and I felt he was with me. When we got to the airport at Milan for me to fly back to London, we said our goodbyes. We didn't know when we would see each other again. I had thought I would be with *The Sound of Music* for about six months in Australia and save enough money to study in Italy with Toti dal Monte. I'd explained all this to Ivano and given him a recording of me singing, so that he knew what I sounded like. He seemed to be bowled over—he had no idea I'd made any recordings and could sing as well as I did!

Eventually I had a letter from him saying that it would be very difficult for him, as an Italian male, to be faithful to me. He had to explain that there would be other women in his life, but he would be waiting for me when I came back, and he would understand if there were other men in my life. This upset me, but I just wrote and said we'd see how it all planned out. We continued writing while I was in Australia, then I had a letter from him saying that my letters upset him so much that he couldn't really enjoy his other girls, so he felt for a while we should stop writing! I was quite desolate. I didn't answer and I put him out of my mind. Then I had a card from him asking me to write to him again, because he missed my letters and he wanted to hear from me. But I didn't – I kept him behind me. As it happened, I suppose it was the best thing because all sorts of things happened to me during *The Sound of Music*'s fifteen-month run. So I would never go back to Italy. *Addio,* Ivano!

When I realised that *The Sound of Music* was obviously going to run for a long while, I asked Faith if she could send me a few extra things that I needed from home. She wrote to say that she had met an officer on the P & O ship *Oriana* who was about due to come out to Australia and he had consented to bring a great suitcase full of things for me. She explained when the ship was docking and said, 'Just ask for Pirelli.' At the docks I first got in touch with the ship's telephone and asked to speak to someone called Pirelli, but nobody knew Pirelli. So I went on board and said I was looking for somebody called Pirelli, who was an officer. Everyone was trying to find Pirelli and then they asked if I could tell them something more about him. I said all I knew was that he's fairly tall, dark, good-looking and thinks he's a lady-killer. They said, 'Oh, you mean Parson.'

'No, I mean Pirelli.'

Eventually he arrived. His name was Peter Parson. I looked at him and said, 'Peter-bloody-Parson! Faith told me your name was Pirelli.'

He said, 'That's just a name that a few people call me.'

I said, 'You're Pirelli to me.'

And he became Pirelli. He had my things there and he invited me down to his cabin for a drink. A few of his friends arrived and we sat round drinking pink gin. He really was very dishy and I fell for him hook, line and sinker, as he did for me – I think!

I saw him a lot while the ship was in dock. Then whenever he was in Sydney we met and we had a lovely romance. He used to write lovely letters to me, telling me all about his family. They sounded absolutely charming. At one of his visits we even talked about marrying, but to my horror I discovered that if I married Pirelli I would have to give up my singing career! He expected me to be there with the dry martinis waiting when he came home. He said he'd give up the sea and take a shore job with P & O—he already had his master's certificate.

I said, 'Peter, I can't do that, I love my career.'

'That's what it will have to be if you marry me.'

That was the end of my lovely romance with Pirelli because there was no way I could give up my career.

Around the same time Richard Finny came into my life. I went to a party on the Sunday afternoon of Australia Day in 1962 with two friends, Lola Brooks, who was playing Elsa Schraeder in *The Sound of Music*, and Michael McGurran, my solicitor. I was feeling the worse for wear after a party the night before, after which I'd sat up for the rest of the night and all of Sunday talking to Lola and Michael. It was a boiling hot day, as well. When we arrived at the party at 4 p.m. I saw a great old leather arm-chair underneath an open window. I aimed for it and said, 'I'm going to sit here and not move. If anyone wants to talk to me, they can come to me.'

Michael got me a drink. Suddenly I looked up and there in the middle of the room I saw a fairly tall young man in profile. The profile was aristocratic, and as I looked closer it seemed very much like the famous portrait of the Duke of Wellington, with the hooked nose. He was smartly dressed in country tweeds, even down to the leather elbows. I was quite impressed by this young man. Eventually someone brought him over and introduced us. He was charming. When I asked him what was in his glass, he said he was drinking scotch and milk. I thought that was an extraordinary drink and said I'd love one. He got me one, then turned away

June having a chat with her former singing teacher, Madame Mathy, on *This is Your Life* in Sydney, 1975.

A scene from the 1975 Australian Opera production of *Rigoletto* with June as Gilda and Reginald Byers as the Duke.

The New Zealand production of *The Merry Widow* in 1975. June (who is 4 ft 11 in) can be seen under the outstretched arm of Danilo, played by Max Cryer (who is 6ft 4 in).

June with her sister Barbara and Rex Wrennall (Freddie) after her investiture with the OBE in April 1977.

One of June's costumes for the South Australian Theatre Company's 1978 production of *Oh, What a Lovely War, Mate!*

Mrs Crawford from the Australian version of *Are You Being Served?*

The cast of the 1982 London production of *The Sound of Music* being presented to Princess Anne. *Left to right:* Honor Blackman, June Bronhill (the Mother Abbess), John Bennett.

June as Ruth in the Australian production of *The Pirates of Penzance* (1984–6).

to talk to other people and knocked the scotch and milk all over me. He had no idea he'd done this.

I left the party with Michael and Lola at 6.30. We were invited to another party a week later, on the Saturday night after the show. I really didn't want to go, nor did Lola, but in the end we went. When we arrived the first person I walked into was this young gentleman. We reintroduced ourselves and I found out his name was Richard Finny. I stayed with him, chatting and laughing, most of the evening. He was a great raconteur with a marvellous sense of humour and wonderful charm. It was then arranged that Lola and I, and he and another dear friend, Freddie Gibson, would have a wonderful Sunday party together. (Freddie is now managing director of Theatre Royal in Sydney but then he was part of the Garnet Carroll organisation.) The party was a riot. Richard arrived with bottles of Veuve Cliquot, scotch, brandy – you name it, he brought it! I thought he must be a wealthy young man! Then he told me he worked for the ABC in television and went on at great length about his family tree. His name was Richard Milburne Champion de Crespigny Finny. I fell about laughing – nobody could have a name like that. He showed me his lovely ring with the family crest. I thought he must be the biggest bullshit artist I'd ever met. But he was great fun. We had a wonderful afternoon and evening.

It was a wonderful relationship. Richard and I immediately hit it off. We became very close. One weekend we were invited to stay with some friends who had a beachhouse at Mt Eliza, outside Melbourne. We drove down after the show. We all enjoyed a wonderful lobster supper and laughed and talked and drank wine. We retired about 2.30 a.m. Richard and I went to bed together and for the first time in my life – I was thirty-two – I was fulfilled sexually. Richard was a very warm lover, a wonderful and generous lover. At about 4.30 in the morning, both of us all aglow, dawn was breaking and we decided to go for a walk down to the beach. As we were walking down a little

169

unsealed road, Richard suddenly stopped. He bent down to pick up a little stone, the perfect shape of a heart. We felt this was our omen. Our love developed from there. Richard was already married but living apart from his wife. I was free. We saw each other quite regularly, as we were both working in Melbourne. Richie would visit me whenever he could, and we would often have little parties for our friends. Everyone liked him because of his incredible charm. When *The Sound of Music* moved to Sydney, Richard came up with me. We moved into a lovely flat in Rose Bay.

After I'd been in Sydney for a while I discovered I was putting on a bit of weight and I was having trouble losing it. Then, in November 1962, I discovered I'd missed a period and I told Richie I thought I was pregnant. Two doctors in Sydney said I wasn't pregnant, but I felt sure I was, so I decided to fly to Melbourne to see my gynaecologist, Dr 'Bung' Hill. Bung told me that without a doubt I was about eleven weeks pregnant. He asked if Richard and I were married and I said we couldn't marry because Richard was still in the throes of a divorce. He said to us both, 'If you don't want to have this child, I can very easily and legally arrange for you to have an abortion because of the fibroids June had six months ago. But I can tell you, if you decide to have this child, it will be a beautiful child, because children conceived purely of love are nine times out of ten the most beautiful children of all. However, I won't try to influence you. This is something you both have to think about. Go away, discuss it and let me know what you decide.'

Richie and I walked away, got half a block, looked at each other and said, 'Let's have the baby; it doesn't matter whether we can be married before it's born or not.' So we immediately went straight back to Bung Hill and told him we'd made up our minds already. He was thrilled! 'I do promise you,' he said, 'it will be beautiful, but apart from that, we will now discuss how you're having this child. June, you must have a caesarian section because you are very small inside and with your myomectomy and the trouble with your retroverted uterus, you couldn't possibly go through a full pregnancy. You would also go through extreme pain and I don't want that. So we'll decide now that you will have the baby three weeks before the proper time.'

We worked out then and there that our child would be born at nine o'clock on the morning of Wednesday 15 May 1963. Richard and I were both over the moon about the whole thing. We didn't know if we could get married in time or not but, as it happened, my solicitor was able to push things along a bit and Richard and I were married on 17 January 1963. Most people fell for a story in which I told the press that I had been secretly married for some months but of course I hadn't been!

When I told everyone in the company that I was leaving the show because I was pregnant there was great jubilation. Everyone was thrilled for me. We made this announcement before we knew whether we could get married. Then we got the OK and on 17 January 1963 I was once again married in a registry office, this time in Macquarie Street, Sydney. At the time both my niece Jaye and my step-daughter from my first marriage, Faith, were living with us. They were our two witnesses. When we all signed the register, there were Richard Milburne Champion de Crespigny Finny, address 351 New South Head Road, Rose Bay; myself, June Mary Martin, known professionally as Bronhill, same address; Faith Josephine Margaret Martin, same address; Marie Jaye Perry, same address. I'm sure the registrar thought Richard was running a house of ill repute! Madame Mathy and her friend, Walter, gave us a wonderful wedding reception and lots of people from *The Sound of Music* cast were there. It was a wonderful day. To top it off, some other dear friends, the McKittrick family, who ran the Log Cabin Hotel out at Penrith, gave us another big wedding reception after the performance that night.

Our baby was born in May and we called her Carolyn Jane, or Biddy for short. I think she is so wonderful that I've given her the whole of the next chapter to herself!

The year before, I'd had fibroids removed from my womb. They had caused three miscarriages I'd had with Brian. Because of this, during my pregnancy I was afraid of Richard making love to me as I didn't want anything to go wrong. I realised later that this was wrong, but at the time it seemed the right thing to do. After I had Biddy, even with everything going well, it was difficult to get back to our usual loving relationship. We still loved each other's company and had wonderfully warm moments, but I found it difficult to get back the old situation between us.

Then I was asked to return to London for the musical, *Robert and Elizabeth*. Luckily Richard got a marvellous job with the BBC as director of BBC2 news, but it kept him away from me for long hours every day and night, and gradually we drifted apart. It was very sad. We still had great affection for each other but we seemed to delight in hurting each other – I don't know why. No matter how much either of us tried to get back on to the old footing, nothing worked. We were both miserable and I could see our marriage falling apart. We had many arguments over absolutely nothing. Naturally, Richard found happiness with other women and when I found that I couldn't get close to him, no matter how I tried, I suppose the only thing left for me was to look elsewhere as well.

In 1968, when I did Ivor Novello's *The Dancing Years*, one of the members of the company playing the role of Franzel was a charming young man called Nicholas Hawtrey. He was both a descendant of the famous Hawtrey actor-management family and a descendant of Ellen Terry. Nicky was divine. He was a Leo and looked every bit a Leo. He was a lion, tall, strong, masculine-looking man, blond, and quite a good actor. He knew a tremendous amount about acting and taught me a lot. He also played the piano quite beautifully and I'm sure if he had had the initiative and ambition, he could have become a fine concert pianist. At first Nicky and I just laughed and chatted together. One night when we were playing in York at the York Theatre, opposite

172

York Minster, I took the principals of the show out to dinner. Nicky turned to me and said, 'You are very generous, June. Next week, when we're in Hull, I would love to take you out to dinner.' Which he did. Nicky was wonderful company. He ordered the food; I was not allowed to even look at the menu. It was really great fun, until it came to paying the bill. Nicky didn't have anywhere near enough money, so he looked at me with his wonderful eyes and said, 'I'm terribly sorry, June, but I don't seem to have brought enough money.' I paid more than half the bill, but I didn't mind!

Nicky and I had a lovely friendship, very loving, very warm and in many ways very fulfilling. A couple of weeks after Hull, we were in Liverpool. Nicky, of course, always walked me back to the hotel. He owned an Alsatian called Greta. This particular night when he was walking me home to the hotel, we came to a very busy intersection. He was striding out and I was trotting along behind him. Just as we got to the corner, a car swerved around and he said, 'Heel.' I almost got down on all fours. But that's how he treated me, rather the way he treated Greta. And I loved it! Nicky asked me if I'd like to go to Ireland for the weekend and fly back to Wolverhampton (where we were performing the following week). I jumped at it—I thought there couldn't be anything more wonderful to do. Our naughty weekend started by driving from Liverpool to Chester, then catching the train to Holyhead and the ferry across to Dun Laoghaire. We started to come into the bay about six o'clock in the morning and it was super. We saw the sun come up and the seagulls were cawing. It was very romantic, a beautiful morning. We took a taxi to the Gresham in Dublin for breakfast.

We were shown a lovely table and started to order our breakfast. Suddenly I became aware of a family sitting at a table in the corner about twenty feet away. They kept looking over and whispering amongst themselves. I turned to Nicky and said, 'I don't know what's going on, but there's a family over there that keeps looking at me. Our dirty

173

weekend is no longer a secret.' He shrieked with laughter. Within fifteen minutes the mother and children came across to us. She said, 'Excuse me, but you are June Bronhill, aren't you?'

'Yes.'

'How wonderful to see you — we're from Melbourne. The children were only very young when they saw you in *The Sound of Music* and we're so thrilled. Will you sign our breakfast menu?'

Nicky and I didn't know where to put ourselves. It was hysterical.

We had a wonderful weekend. Nicky showed me the most marvellous places. We bought almost matching sweaters in Aran knit. When we arrived in Wolverhampton, it was bitterly cold. The company saw us arrive at the theatre in our sweaters and they all knew where we'd been! Nicky and I had a lovely romance, one that will remain in my heart for ever.

In 1970 things were still pretty grim between Richard and me. Nothing that either of us did made matters any happier. I was asked to do Noël Coward's *Bitter Sweet*. The morning of the first rehearsal, I walked in and looked round the company thinking, 'Now, who can I flirt with? They're all gay, they're all pretty boys. Oh well, what the hell.' I looked up and saw one charming man whom I found out later was playing the villain in *Bitter Sweet*, the evil baron. He was sitting doing the *Daily Telegraph* cryptic crossword puzzle. I am a cryptic crossword puzzle fanatic, so I sat next to him and said, 'It's John Marsden, isn't it?'

'Yes.'

'Do you like these puzzles?'

He said he adored them. So we did a couple of clues together and I said, 'Anybody available here?'

'I don't think so, darling. I think they're all a bit the other way.'

'Oh well, it doesn't matter. What about that nice young man over there?' (I must admit I was old enough to be his mother!)

'I think that's Tony Rowlands. No luck there, June.'

We finished our rehearsal period in London before the tour, and everyone was getting along well. It was a very happy company. We'd been away for a few weeks and one night I said to our company manager, Gerry Phillips, 'I need a little bit of a kiss and a cuddle, but there's nobody who would fancy me.'

'Get away, young Rowlands over there thinks you're marvellous.'

'I thought he was gay.'

After that Ant Rowlands, as I got to know him, and I became very dear friends. He was wonderful to me throughout that tour. He looked after me, always made sure I was in the right place at the right time. I'd arrive in my dressing-room in each new theatre and there, in something like an old milk bottle, would be a beautiful rose or carnation and a card, 'From Ant'. He was absolutely lovely and we became very close to each other. When we got back to London he stayed with me. By now my inevitable divorce was going through and I was living at home in Knightsbridge with Biddy and Ant. One day he said he was going home to see his parents and asked me down for the weekend. They lived in Essex, in a village called Kirby Le Soken, not far from Frinton. I met his parents, Len and Sue – divine people! They were a marvellous family. Quite regularly Ant would take Biddy and me down there for weekends and we had wonderful time together. Biddy and I had many lovely Christmases with them after Richard and I had broken up.

One weekend when we were down there Sue and Len just suddenly looked at each other and then at us and almost as one, said, 'Why don't you two get married?' Ant and I just fell about with laughter. I was forty and Ant was twenty-two. Can you imagine what it would have been like when he was forty and I was fifty-eight? We said, 'No. We are wonderfully good friends, we appreciate each other's company and have a great warmth and great affection for each other, but that's it!' I'm very happy to say that we still are friends to this day.

Ant, by the way, was a very good actor. After we'd finished *Bitter Sweet*, he got a job with the Lincoln Repertory Company and I saw him act in some wonderful plays. I think he was perhaps the best Romeo I've ever seen. He was the right age and had all the natural youth and energy required for the role. He has so much talent but never made it, for some extraordinary reason. He also wrote plays, very funny one-acters. I look back on those days when we were the dearest of dear friends with a lot of joy and a lot of love.

After that my love life, if you can call it that, was pretty quiet until I came back to Australia for the Australian Opera Company in 1976. In that season I played Rosina in *The Barber of Seville*, Blonde in *Il Seraglio*, Gilda in *Rigoletto* and in the Gilbert and Sullivan season I played Josephine in *HMS Pinafore* and Phyllis in *Iolanthe*. During the Gilbert and Sullivan season I had noticed this young man flitting round in tight jeans, T-shirts and lovely tan boots up to his knees. We would smile at each other but nobody ever introduced us. I hadn't a clue who he was but I liked him, I liked his personality—he was a bit like me, a bit cheeky! One day, in between a matinee and the evening performance, I remembered that I had a wardrobe query. I saw the wardrobe master, Ray Godden, talking to this young man. I said to Ray, 'I want to see you about one of my costumes—something that needs fixing up. Will you come and see me before the show tonight?'

'Yes, of course, June.'

'While you're here, will you introduce me to this young man? I've seen him around and nobody has introduced us.'

He introduced me and the young man said, 'My name is Rex,' but I thought he said, 'My name is Fred' so I said, 'Oh, isn't that lovely! I've got a cat in London called Fred.'

'My name's not Fred, it's Rex.'

'Well, that's bad luck, because from now on you're going to be Fred.'

He told me his name was Rex Wrennall and he also told me that he had fallen in love with me in *The Dancing Years* in Eastbourne. I said, 'What do you mean?'

'As you've no doubt gathered from my accent, I come from England. I was working in the lighting department of *The Dancing Years* and I just thought you were the most marvellous thing.' So we became extremely good friends then and there.

The most extraordinary thing was that I found out that Freddie came from Preston in Lancashire and my dear friend Marjorie Roscoe was also from Preston. Who should come up and talk to us at that moment but Edgar Metcalfe, a wonderful actor and director who also comes from Preston! I said, 'After the show tonight, everyone comes back to my place and we'll phone Marjorie.' So these three Lancashire people had a marvellous three-way conversation in my flat in Elizabeth Bay in Sydney. It was hysterical. If we'd had another phone we'd have had a four-way conversation. We had Marje in London, the boys at my place on the two phones and me chipping in! We had a wonderful time. Freddie didn't go home that night and that was the start of my last lovely love affair!

The loving part of it lasted, I suppose, about two years, but the more important part of it, the friendship, has lasted ten years. We have the most incredible rapport. We have similar senses of humour; we understand each other to the point that it's quite uncanny. I'll open my mouth to say something and Freddie will say it and *vice versa*. I'll be away on tour and pick up the phone to phone him and the phone will be engaged; I'll hang up and the phone will ring – it will be his nibs. We'll think exactly the same way about how we should plan a day, a week, my career, his life and career, meals. In a kitchen we are amazing together – we come up with the most magical meals and, as with Richard, Freddie and I give marvellous parties. Not only has he been my dear friend, my lover and, in many ways, my mentor but he has also managed my business affairs, and made some of the most fantastic concert gowns for me. I don't think anybody has understood me quite as well as Freddie has. How he puts

177

up with me sometimes I don't know, and conversely, how I put up with him sometimes, I don't know. But we have a relationship that I'm sure many people would envy.

Here endeth the so-called sex life of a so-called prima donna. I've loved so many people but perhaps the reason why I've never settled down and stuck with any one person is because I've never really been *in* love with any of them. I think, perhaps, there are only three things that I am *in* love with, my career, my public and my darling daughter.

13

Carolyn Jane

Richard and I discussed names for our baby and immediately decided that a boy would be Charles Richard. If the baby were a girl we decided to name her after Richard's great-great-grandmother, who had been Lady Carolyn Jane de Crespigny. Then, just before I went into hospital, the doctor said he could feel arms and legs all over the place, so we thought maybe they were going to be twins and they had to be twin boys. We called them Archie and Charles for want of better names!

Eventually my time came to go into hospital. On the morning of my caesarian I'd been given my medication and everything was ready for the birth at nine o'clock. I was very dopey and couldn't work out why I still hadn't been taken into the operating theatre. Then the nursing sister said,'We're very sorry, June, but we have to wait a little while because we've just had a phone call from the paediatrician to say he's been caught in a traffic jam and will be here as soon as possible.' They couldn't re-sedate me, because it would have been bad for the child. So I just waited, and hoped he'd get there reasonably quickly.

At about 9.20 on the morning of Wednesday, 15 May 1963, Carolyn Jane Finny came into my life. She weighed 6 lb 7 oz. When I came out of the theatre, Bung Hill said,'It's a girl, June, and she's absolutely beautiful.' I just smiled. As I was being wheeled to my room, Richie was waiting for me and he said, 'It's a girl, darling, and she's absolutely beautiful.' They both said the same thing!

'I'm sorry we haven't got our boys,' I said.

'Who cares about the boys? We've got our darling girl and she's lovely.'

179

And she was. She was as pretty as a picture with lovely brown eyes and brown hair, and a chubby little face. She had a little smile on her face all the time and I could have sworn she could see, though I knew, of course, that she couldn't.

One day, when she was just a little out of sorts, I decided I'd just sing 'Edelweiss' from *The Sound of Music* to her. It worked like a charm, so after that whenever she was slightly miserable, which wasn't very often, 'Edelweiss' came to the fore.

We were in hospital for about two and a half weeks before I was allowed to take her home. At home she suddenly made funny little clucking noises, just like a little chicken, so Richard started calling her Chicken and from Chicken, I called her Chickabiddy. By the time she was three weeks old, the Chicka part had gone and she'd just become Biddy. She's been Biddy ever since to the family.

As she grew older she definitely wanted to be called by her proper name. Not the full Carolyn Jane, which I thought was beautiful, and I'd have loved to call her, but Carolyn as she was to her friends. Recently I asked if she would like me to call her Carolyn now. She said, 'Dear God, no, it would sound so silly—you and Dad and all the members of the family and certain special friends, I couldn't bear them calling me Carolyn. I'm Biddy to you and that's what I want to stay.'

She really was a divine baby, except that not long after we came home from hospital, I discovered she was becoming grizzly and didn't seem to be satisfied in some way. After one day of complete crying, I said to Richard, 'Please, darling, go out and buy her some dummies.' So we boiled up the dummies and she became a dummy baby. A lot of people think that is bad, bad for their teeth and a load of other old wives' tales—but I just went ahead using them. After about a week I took her to see the paediatrician. He said she was not getting a strong enough mixture (I was not feeding her myself), and that even though it shouldn't be stepped up just yet, he thought I must do so and give her a little more. That was it! She was as happy as a sandgirl after that. She never cried; she was a happy, delightful child. She flourished! She adored having her photo taken. From the time she was about three months old, if she saw a camera coming within cooee, the little smile was all there. She rather takes after her mother in that way. She was really quite the most enchanting child and everybody loved her. She loved music, too. She used to go to sleep at night listening to Beethoven's 9th Symphony, her favourite music. We even used to catch her 'conducting', as we said, because her little arms were going in time with the music.

As she grew she developed lovely habits. She adored coming to the theatre, even when she was a baby. I returned to work when she was about five months old, doing a return season of *The Merry Widow* for Garnet Carroll and as we didn't have a nanny, she came to the theatre with me in a bassinet and often slept through the noise of the Tannoy system in my dressing-room. Sometimes, if she woke up, one of the girls who was not on stage would look after her and even carry her out into the wings so she could be held there. She was fascinated by the music and lights and dancing. I thought, 'We've got another one in the family like me.'

As she grew up she remained fascinated by music and painting. When she was about three or four she used to come home from nursery school with paintings to show me. Of course I didn't have a clue what they were of. Her first effort was quite extraordinary. It was a myriad of colours, blues and lilacs, but in the middle was a gingery colour. I said, 'That's absolutely beautiful, darling. What is it?'

She retorted, 'It's a teddy bear, of course!'

I felt so small not recognising a teddy bear.

When she was about two and a half she became quite interested in going to the bathroom whenever Richard was in there and giving him a fairly close scrutiny. One day she said, 'Daddy, what's that?' pointing to you-know-what.

'Well, darling, um, er, that's Daddy's thing.'

'Oh, I see.'

181

That was the end of that conversation, so Richard thought. But after being asked the same question a few times, Richard became exasperated and said, 'I've told you it's Daddy's thing. Where's Biddy's thing?'

'Oh, Daddy,' she said, 'girls don't have things, they have fannies.'

Richard was quite nonplussed.

Richie, who really has got a devil of a sense of humour, tried to teach her a variation on a nursery rhyme. He kept saying it to her over and over again trying to get her to repeat it and the nursery rhyme was:

Little Miss Muffett sat on her tuffett,
Early one summer's morn
It wasn't the spider that sat down beside her,
It was Little Boy Blue with his horn.

She never ever tried to repeat it – not once. Lisa, the girl who was looking after her at this time, took her to a parents' day at her nursery school. I was doing a matinee and couldn't go. All the children were getting up and doing their party pieces. In the past, whenever she'd been asked to do anything, she would get very shy and wouldn't do it, but lo and behold, this particular afternoon she suddenly put her hand up and said she wanted to recite. She got up and went through Richard's rhyme, word-perfectly! She shattered everybody, particularly Lisa, who didn't know where to look.

Quite often, when she was four and five, if I was asked to go to a function, a morning or afternoon 'do' or cut a tape to open something, but I was too busy with my work, I'd say I was sorry but I couldn't possibly do it. Then they'd say, 'Could your little daughter come along?' I'd tell them she couldn't make speeches, but they'd say it didn't matter, that it would be lovely to have somebody there who was associated with me. I would say, 'I don't know how she'll behave but OK.' She opened one toy fair, which was great fun, and we have marvellous photos of her cutting the tape and full of bubble and energy. Everybody simply adored her.

182

She went to another luncheon attended by lots of local dignitaries, including the Governor of Victoria's wife. Biddy was at the top table, sitting next to Her Excellency, and Lisa was right down the other end of the main table. Suddenly, in the middle of the lunch, Biddy leant across the table and called, 'Lisa, I want to do big jobbies.' That almost put an end to the luncheon!

When we were settled back in London when she was about five, she used to adore listening to classical music and would sing along with whatever record we played. Although she didn't know the piece, she would always be in tune, almost as if she knew the music. She would also sing an octave higher! I really thought we had a singer on our hands, because she really had the most pure, beautiful, natural voice I think I've ever heard. It might have been what I sounded like when I was her age! Of course, I had the wonderful influence of my father playing piano for me and having sing-songs around the piano which Biddy didn't have. She really was fascinated by singing. One night we were sitting watching a girl singing on television and Biddy was sitting on the floor at my feet, listening. She would look at me and I thought, 'I won't say anything. I'll let her eventually ask me whatever is on her mind.' After looking at me several times she asked, 'Mummy, what do you think of that voice?'

I said, 'Why don't you tell me what you think of it.'

'It's a bit crooked.'

And she was right! The girl's voice had quite a wide vibrato. I said she was right and she asked me what made it crooked. I explained things like not breathing correctly, and sometimes pressing the voice too hard to try to attain an effect. A couple of times after that, when I was bathing her and getting her ready for bed and singing away, she'd look at me and say, 'Mummy, that's a bit crooked. Be careful.' She always knew!

Another time, while we were watching some skating on television, the young man went into a wonderful fast spin. Biddy looked up at me and said, 'You know, if he's not careful, he's going to turn himself into butter.' And at the ripe old age of two and a half she was referring to those after-dinner mints called 'After Eights' as 'Before Nines'. I don't know how she worked it out, but she was quite right again.

She loved dancing and when she was six I enrolled her in the Rambert Ballet School in London. A couple of her school chums were also having ballet lessons and they always came to our place to play and dance. About three or four of these little girls would come home a couple of times a week and would make up their own plays. One day they got a recording out of orchestral excerpts from Bizet's *Carmen*. They said, 'June, will you put this record on, please?' (They all called me June.) They absolutely fell in love with the music of *Carmen*, so of course I had to tell them the story of the opera. I explained what each section of the orchestra related to as far as what was occurring in the opera. They sat down on their own for fifteen minutes and choreographed their *Carmen*. They had to double up on some parts, but they had it all worked out in their minds. It was really very imaginative. This was all great fun for me, too. I thought maybe this daughter of mine would be a ballet dancer or a singer, and then I discovered, too, that she had the most delightful sense of humour. In some of the plays they made up, she was incredibly funny. The awful thing for me was that I was supposed to give them points out of ten and even though I think most times Biddy was the best, I very rarely let her win. I gave all the encouragement to the others. She'd say to me afterwards, 'I thought I was a bit better than Claire.' I'd say, 'Well, you were pretty good, Bid, but the others were very good too, and we must always give people encouragement, mustn't we?' I think that pacified her!

During school holidays Biddy would come on tour with us, particularly when I was doing the Noël Coward and Ivor Novello musicals.

In the 1970s a young touring company called the Basicila Opera Company asked me whether I'd be interested in doing some performances of Violetta in *La Traviata* by Verdi. I

Norman Yem as the Mikado and June as Katisha from *The Mikado*, Melbourne, 1985.

June as the Duchess of Plaza-Toro in *The Gondoliers*, Melbourne, 1985.

'My name's Pauline, but most people call me Paul.'
A challenging role for June in *Women Behind Bars*
in Sydney, 1985.

Madonna and child. June and her daughter Carolyn in 1983.

Freddie and June with Dora.

Carolyn and Brian, 1987.

jumped at that because I had studied the role with my darling Dino Borgioli but had never been asked to sing it. I worked hard on the role. Biddy, who was about nine at the time, came with me. She said she wanted to watch the dress rehearsal, and I said, 'Be careful after the performance that you don't get in anybody's way.' After the rehearsal finished, we had a bit of a discussion on stage, then I went to my dressing-room. I opened my door and couldn't see Biddy anywhere. Then I realised she was standing behind the door, crying.

'What on earth's the matter?' I asked.

'Nothing.'

'Did you do something wrong backstage? Did you get in someone's way?'

'Oh, no,' to which I replied that there must be something wrong for her to be sobbing. She answered that when she saw me die, at first she thought I really had died and it made her realise how she would feel when I did die! I discussed with her whether she wanted to sit out front and see the opening night. She thought for a while and said, 'No, I don't think so.'

The following day, however, she came to me and said, 'I think I should go and see it again, because it will make me get used to seeing you die.' I thought that was sweet.

Sadler's Wells approached me in 1972 and asked if I would like to do *The Merry Widow*, just one performance at the Coliseum, then on tour. I said I'd love to and that I'd come and see the production. Biddy and I sat in a box at the back of the auditorium. The girl who was playing the Widow was a lovely performer with a good voice, but she was on the plump side. She wore a costume with a grey satin underskirt which emphasised her bottom when she walked. At one stage she had to walk up some steps with her back to the audience. Biddy looked at her, then turned to me and looked back again. Suddenly, it was too much for her. She said, 'Mummy, she's even fatter than you are!' I decided there and then that I would not wear that costume!

185

When we were on tour Biddy would also help the principal ladies to dress. One of these was a wonderful actress called Barbara Miller, and one day Barbara said to me, 'Biddy is quite extraordinary. She is helping me with quick changes in the wings and I only have to tell her once exactly how I want things given to me and she does it. She's absolutely perfect – better than a lot of the professional dressers. She never flurries, never gets in my way, and knows exactly when to get away from me when I have to go on stage!'

A couple of weeks later Barbara said to me, 'I have to tell you this. I was changing in the dressing-room and Biddy said to me, "Miss Miller, I hope you don't think I'm being rude, but do you know in the last scene you said some wrong words?" She then told me what I had said, followed by what I should have said – and she was exactly right!'

Barbara told me she'd had a bit of a mental block and made up a few words. Biddy had picked it up straightaway. She only had to hear something a few times to memorise it.

Biddy said to me one day, 'Mummy, if I really worked at it, I could be a dresser when I grow up.'

'You just could, darling, and I'll tell you what, good dressers are very hard to find and they are the most important thing for we people on stage.' I went on to tell her about some of the wonderful dressers that I've had. They do everything for you. They see your make-up is in good clean order; you don't have to say your dressing-gown needs washing, or something needs ironing. They go over your costumes every night, and there is never anything wrong. I told her that a good dresser is worth her weight in gold.

Biddy has a great sensitivity. When I was getting ready to go to South Africa to do *Robert and Elizabeth*, Richard and I were at the stage where things were not going well for us. One day we had had a really nasty row. I lost my temper and was upstairs crying, pulling things out of drawers and starting to pack and putting them back in and not knowing what to do. Biddy came into me and said, 'Don't cry, Mummy. In a few weeks you'll be in South Africa and you'll be away from all this.' Of course it made things worse—I was a blubbering idiot after that!

A lot of people say that one should hold on to a marriage because of the children, but I think they don't realise how sensitive the children are, and that children *do* know when things are not going well. I could see that Richard's and my arguing was really rubbing off on her and she was getting in quite a mental turmoil. She loved us both dearly, but it's awful for a child to see parents not as happy as they used to be. After we'd divorced, she was an entirely different child. She realised it was for the better as far as we were concerned, and it certainly was for the better as far as she was concerned in my eyes. I did have custody of her, but the lovely thing about our divorce was that we remained very good friends. There was never any fighting over Biddy. Even when Richard married again we were still, all of us, good friends. When I decided to send Biddy to boarding school, Richard and Bunty (his new wife) and I and Biddy, all went to see the school, so that Biddy could see what she thought of it. I'm sure that sort of thing doesn't happen very often!

The school, St Christopher's, was co-ed and a wonderful place, set in about twenty-six acres of its own land. The children didn't wear uniforms and they called the teachers by their Christian names. If a child showed talent in a particular field, such as music or science, they would encourage that talent. It really was a very sensible form of education. The school turned out to be vegetarian. We didn't say anything about this to Biddy when we took her there to meet the headmistress. When Biddy said she liked the school and the headmistress said she'd love to have her, we said, 'There's one thing we have to tell you—it's vegetarian.'

'What does that mean?' she asked.

'It means you don't have any meat—you just live on fruit and vegetables and things made from vegetables.'

She thought for a while and said, 'Well, I'll just have to get used to it, won't I?'

She took to boarding school life very well. I used to visit her practically every other weekend, staying at a local hotel. Saturday morning was always fun. Biddy and about four of her best friends used to come out with me. I bought them little bits and pieces they wanted. One day Biddy asked me to buy her a torch. I asked why and she said, 'So I can read in bed after lights out,' so I ended up buying them all torches. I'd take them to a restaurant. Each week it was something different – they loved Chinese food, so we'd do that; another time we'd go to a steakhouse; another time to a chicken place; another time spaghetti; so they got their little treats of meat or chicken whenever I came up to see them.

When I was coming out to Australia to do some concerts in Melbourne in January 1975, Richard and Bunty (who were now living in New Zealand) asked us to come out a week earlier and have Christmas with them in Auckland. I thought it was a lovely idea for Biddy to see her father. She hadn't seen him for about eighteen months.

All went swimmingly until Christmas Eve, when they hit me with the biggest thunderbolt imaginable. Richard said he and Bunty would very much like Biddy to live with them in New Zealand for a year. I said that I couldn't uproot her from school just for a year. I didn't think I'd get her back into St Christopher's afterwards, and I was afraid they would end up having her for the rest of her schooling. He and Bunty agreed that would be fine. I said, 'It's for Biddy to decide. She's eleven and a half and old enough to know her own mind, so I'll see just what she says.' Blow me down, when I put the question to her, she said she'd love to live in New Zealand. I was dreadfully upset, because I couldn't imagine not having Biddy with me at home in London. Even though she was at boarding school, I used to see her regularly. But it was her decision and I had to abide by it.

She also had grandparents (Richard's parents), aunties, uncles and cousins in New Zealand, so in many ways it was better for her. As it turned out, all my work in Australia just snowballed suddenly and Biddy would have had to be uprooted from school in any case. Eventually I decided in 1976 to make Australia my home again. So it all turned out for the best.

Biddy has been in New Zealand all this time. She was not academic really, and I still thought she might work in the theatre because she loved it whenever she came over to see me in Australia. She loved seeing the workings backstage. I thought if I could get her into NIDA (the National Institute for Dramatic Art in Sydney), she could do a stage-management course which covers lighting, stage production, direction and so on. She was interested, but whenever she got back to New Zealand she got back into what I called (and I hope my New Zealand readers won't think I'm rude) the NZ rut, the way of life back there. So now she doesn't have anything to do with the theatre. Whenever I see her, if we're going to a party or restaurant where they have a piano playing, she'll always say, 'You won't sing, will you?' which is rather amusing, because over the years she began to realise that her mother was fairly well known!

When she was about seventeen, she was visiting her boyfriend's family when something came up about Biddy's mother being a singer. Someone who was from Australia said, 'Really? Who's your mother?'

'June Bronhill.'

And the visitor said, 'Your mother's June Bronhill?' and turned to the family and said, 'She's one of our most famous singers. Everybody adores her – she's marvellous.'

Biddy said, 'I really felt quite chuffed. I went up in everybody's estimation because you were Bronhill.'

Over the years Biddy has grown even more beautiful. She has a lovely nature, but is shy in many ways, which is probably why she never wants me to sing at restaurants or parties! She's warm and loving, and I cannot believe that I am blessed with such a joy. She now has a good job in Auckland, where she's happy and doing well. She plays the field slightly as far as young men are concerned, and I keep saying, 'When are you going to get married? I want to be a Grannie.'

She says, 'I don't know, Mother. I'm not really interested in all that.'

189

'Do, please. I can't wait to have a lovely little grandson or daughter to spoil the way I spoilt you.'

And believe you me, I did spoil her and I still do and she's worth every bit of it. She is still the only person or thing in this world that I would give up my singing career for. If she suddenly needed me, no matter what I was doing, I would down tools and be there – that's how precious she is.

14

My Adoring Public

Without the public and the fans, those people waiting at the stage-door, or talking to us in the street, we people on the stage would be nothing. Those people are all-important to us performers, and over the years I have gathered many fans, who have eventually become friends, to my bosom.

My first dear fan was Janet Lewis. Janet used to come to all the operas at Sadler's Wells. She had her favourite performers and I was one of the lucky ones. I never quite knew what Janet was going to say to me next, because she was completely honest. She wouldn't say, 'Oh, you were absolutely marvellous, June,' if she thought I was absolutely rotten. As a matter of fact, I remember many occasions when I'd come out of the stage-door at the end of a performance and Janet would be waiting for me, along with another dear fan and friend, Mary Driscoll. There were a few of them, our gallery-ites. I wouldn't say anything but I could tell straightaway, just by the look on Janet's face what was coming. Maybe she'd say, 'That was great tonight, great, better than last week,' or conversely, 'No, didn't sing as well tonight. Sorry about that, June, you really didn't; last week's was much better!' She was wonderful and I always knew that what Janet said was right. There were no trimmings, no great hoo-hah about things; it was down to earth and straight from the gut.

Over the years Janet and Mary kept up a wonderful correspondence with me, particularly when I was back in Australia. They would always let me know what was going on, who was singing this, who was singing that, whether they were singing well or whether they weren't. They really did become very special friends of mine.

191

Another dear friend and fan at that time was Jane Roberts. Jane worked for Anna Neagle and it was through Jane that I first met Anna, who over the years became a close dear friend of mine; what a wonderful lady Dame Anna was. Jane would come to see me whenever she could find time. She loved being part of this new thing for her, opera. Jane became a very good friend and we wrote lots of long letters to each other; this was in the days when I used to write letters! I'm dreadful these days, I'm afraid. So I hope people will forgive me because I haven't been a good correspondent.

There was a wonderful character, David Penney, who used to come down on his motorbike from the Midlands for special performances when he had the night off, then ride back afterwards. He was in one of the forces. David was marvellous. On opening nights, when we'd naturally have first-night parties, I'd leave the theatre at about one o'clock and David would be there, sitting outside on his bike, just waiting to say hullo to me. He was very loyal. Many years later, when I was in Australia, I was doing one of a series of Sunday afternoon concerts in the Myer Music Bowl in Melbourne. I was being driven home after the concert when I looked out the window and I couldn't believe my eyes. There was David Penney. I wound the window down and said, 'It's David, isn't it?'

He said, 'You remember my name! I haven't seen you for years.'

'Of course I remember your name.'

David was absolutely bowled over by this. He said he was living in Australia now.

I said, 'I guess I'll see you sometime.'

'Wherever you're singing, June, I'll be there.' And that's how it is. When I'm in Melbourne, no matter where I'm singing, there is David Penney waiting for me, but never infringing my privacy—just waiting outside until I eventually come out of the stage-door.

I haven't been able to remember Diane's surname. Diane used to sit in the front row of nearly every performance I did of the lovely Ivor Novello shows and Noël Coward's *Bitter Sweet*, back in the early 1970s. One night she came backstage after the performance to see me. She said, 'I hope you don't mind, Miss Bronhill, but I've made this dress for you.'

'But how could you make a dress for me, Diane? You haven't got my measurements.'

'Well, I've looked at you from out front and I think I know.' She gave me this lovely peachy-pink wool crepe dress which fitted me perfectly. It was a loose-fitting style dress but the shoulders, length, sleeves, every part of it was absolutely perfect. I was thrilled and thanked her.

Then, blow me down, a couple of weeks later I walked on to the stage to see Diane sitting in the front row with the identical dress on – she'd made another one for herself! I was highly delighted, though, that I hadn't worn mine that night so we wouldn't have looked like the Dolly Sisters after the show. Then she started copying whatever hairstyle I had, not only in my private life, but in my shows, and copying my costumes! When I did *Glamorous Night*, in the gypsy wedding scene I wore a beautiful gypsy dress. Sure enough, there, in the front row, was Diane wearing a replica of it with the same hairstyle. They say imitation is the sincerest form of flattery, so I guess that was very nice of her! I was awful to her once, though. The performances Diane had attended had been on the South Coast, down in Eastbourne, Brighton or London, as she lived not far from Brighton. Then, blow me down, after an opening night in Birmingham, she knocked on my dressing-room door. When she opened the door, I asked, 'What the bloody hell are you doing up here in Birmingham?'

'I took a week off from work. I wanted to come up and see you, and see the show again.'

'You're out of your mind, girl – think of the money it's costing you.'

'I don't care – I wanted to see you.'

A lot of the kids in the company thought she must have

been in love with me! But I think it was just hero – or heroine – worship. I'm sorry I yelled at her.

While I was with Sadler's Wells I started getting some marvellous photographs from a man called Tank Carpenter, a fellow Australian. Tank used to sit up in the gallery and do something quite illegal – take photographs of the performances. Eventually I met Tank whom I liked immensely. I have some marvellous photographs which I'd never have had otherwise, even if the taking of them was against all the rules. I'm grateful to Tank for the photos and the memories they bring back.

In Australia there was the incredible trio – Michael, Don and Geoff. These three would come to so many of my performances and they were loyal, loving friends and fans. Dear Don McLeod was incredible. He gave me the most beautiful presents. For instance, when I was doing *Robert and Elizabeth,* he found the tiniest copy of Elizabeth Barrett's *Sonnets from the Portuguese* for me. It must have been of Victorian or Edwardian vintage and was quite beautiful. When I was doing the title role in the opera *Maria Stuarda* he gave me a beautiful miniature of Mary Stuart. It was quite enchanting. He would come to Saturday matinees and after the performance, he and the boys would come around to see me. Donny would have a lovely big box of flowers from his garden for me, things like daphne and boronia, beautiful sweet-smelling flowers. They were absolutely gorgeous. They would last me the whole week and my house always looked absolutely beautiful, thanks to Don. When Don died, in his will he left me the most beautiful Meissen plate which depicts Orpheus and Eurydice. It has pride of place in my china cabinet. I still see Michael and Geoff quite regularly and there are a couple of other dear friends of the same group who still come to see me whenever I perform in Melbourne.

Then there's the darling Dorothy Hutchinson. She met me, same as the boys did, when I first came back to do *The Merry Widow.* Dorothy is the most marvellous knitter I've ever known. She would arrive at the theatre with a sweater or something similar for me. Then, a few years later, when I was pregnant, Dorothy knitted some of the most fantastic baby clothes for me. I think everything knitted for the baby (apart from a few things I did myself) was knitted by Dorothy. She made me the most wonderful shawl which I absolutely treasured. Dorothy, like me, has a great love for cats. Every time she sends me a card, whether it be for an opening night or Christmas or my birthday, it will be a lovely card with cats on it!

Another dear friend and fan I met during *The Sound of Music* was Ted O'Donnell. Ted's another one of these people who, every now and then, will send a letter or a card or will phone. We meet occasionally and have lots of laughs about *Sound of Music* days. Ted is another fan who never really intrudes. He's a gem; he understands me very well; he doesn't expect a lot of me, which is wonderful, because when one works as hard as we do in the theatre, there are those times when, really, all we want is to be on our own, just to be at home, relax and be ourselves.

Another of my dear Australian fan-friends is Judy Whyte. Judy has been to every show that I've done for absolutely years. Quite often she brings her Mum and Dad, who are also dears. Mrs Whyte often sends me beautiful hand-painted gifts which I treasure. As a matter of fact, sometimes after a performance, when there may be six or seven people in my dressing-room — most of whom I don't know very well — Judy will be the one who starts the ball rolling by dropping the hint to the others and starting to leave. I often wish there were more sensitive people like Judy Whyte about!

Once at Sydney Airport I bumped into a good friend of mine, Jan Adele, with whom I had worked on television. With her was that wonderful singer, Kathryn Grayson. There were we, three singers, Jan in a natural ranch mink, Kathryn in a white mink and me in a black mink, all looking a million dollars! I had never met Kathryn Grayson before but naturally had seen most of her movies and was a great admirer of hers. We threw our arms round each other and started chatting. Kathryn and I were introduced and we both said we felt we'd known each other for years; then Kathryn said, 'I've got to tell you this, June; I am a great fan of yours. Do you know that I have got lots of your records at home in the States?' I thought that was terrific! I didn't think she would have heard of me. So I think I can count her as a fan, and she can count me as one of hers, as well.

Back in 1958, after a performance of *The Merry Widow* at Sadler's Wells a man called Geoffrey Pretious came backstage to see me. I didn't know him at all, but I allowed him to come into the dressing-room. He started rattling on about how marvellous he thought I was and that he had presents for me. There was a lovely pearl necklace in one parcel and a watch in the other. I said, 'I'm sorry, Mr Pretious, I can't possibly accept these gifts; they cost a lot of money.'

He said, 'When I first started hearing you sing I decided I'd give up smoking, and I've just bought these gifts out of the money that I've saved from not smoking.'

'That's very kind of you, and I'm glad that I've stopped you smoking, but I really cannot accept them.'

Well, a lot of hooing and hahaing went on, and in the end I thought I'd better accept them, but I begged him never to do anything like that again. Occasionally he came backstage to see me and there were no presents. Then one night he said to me, 'Tell me, Miss Bronhill, what perfume do you like?' I really didn't have a clue, because in those days I was not really a perfume user, but somebody had told me about a new perfume by Fabergé called Woodhue, so off the top of my head, I said, 'Oh, I really do quite like Fabergé Woodhue.' About a week later he came to see me and said, 'I'm dreadfully sorry, I've tried all over London to get Woodhue, but it isn't available anywhere here. Harrods told me that Fabergé only makes it for the American market, so it's only on sale in Paris and in America.'

'It's very kind of you to go to all that trouble, but forget it.'

Two weeks later he arrived and said, 'Do you know where I've been this weekend?'

'No, Mr Pretious, I haven't got the faintest idea.'

'I've been to Paris.'

'What on earth for?'

'I went to get your Woodhue.'

'This is ridiculous! You shouldn't do these things.'

'I want you to have whatever you want.'

I was becoming embarrassed by all of this and said, 'Please, in the future, don't do things like this because it is very embarrassing for me.'

Mr Pretious was a short meek-looking man, not at all like your Stagedoor Johnny! He was a very ordinary little man and looked as if he didn't have two pennies to rub together. Lo and behold, a parcel arrived for me at Sadler's Wells, direct from Fabergé in Paris. It contained not only Woodhue perfume but the toilet water, dusting powder with a lovely big puff, talcum powder, bathcubes, soap—every conceivable type of product—small perfume sprays for handbags—you name it, it was there.

It must have cost him a fortune. When I saw him next I said, 'You know, it's very very kind of you but, please, it must stop.' Well, of course, it didn't. Every four weeks I'd get another great big package of products from Fabergé, to the extent that in the end I just said to him, 'I've got so much perfume and powder and soap and talc that I really cannot cope with any more.' But still they came. In the end I was keeping everybody at Sadler's Wells in Woodhue and I realised I didn't even really like it! Of course I couldn't say *that* to Geoffrey.

Then I went home to Australia to do *The Merry Widow* and while I was there all sorts of lovely things arrived at the theatre for me. When I went back to London I was on my own, having divorced Brian. Geoffrey, I think, thought he was going to step into Brian's shoes and just pestered me like there was no tomorrow! While I was charming to him, to me he was no more than a devoted fan. All this went on

197

for another nine months until I went to Australia in 1961 to do *The Sound of Music*. I think Geoffrey was rather horrified when I met and married Richard. All the time, beautiful presents arrived in Australia for me – wonderful negligees and nightgowns – Richard said naughty things about these! – bed jackets, still the perfume, handkerchiefs, nylons, you name it, I got it from Geoffrey Pretious. Then, of course, when I arrived back in London in 1964 I had my darling daughter with me and my new husband, but he was not deterred in the least. Beautiful presents arrived for Biddy, absolutely gorgeous clothes. This man had perfect taste. One outfit for Biddy was a most beautiful red velvet coat, trimmed with white mink with a little matching hat. It must have cost him a lot of money; Geoffrey wouldn't be stopped by anything I said or did. From that time every Saturday I received a hamper containing a capon, or a chicken, a bottle of champagne, a tin of ham, a wonderful jar of either cherries jubilee, apricots in brandy or plums in champagne, and there would also be half a bottle of cognac; literally everything I could need for a Sunday meal, with the exception of the vegetables. Every weekend this happened. When I was doing *Robert and Elizabeth,* apart from weekend hampers, on matinee days he would bring me a meal of salmon and salad from Fortnum and Masons between shows.

One day, when all of this had been going on for seven years, Geoffrey asked me to have tea with him and his sister at their home. I was able to cope with him after the occasional performance but I didn't see how I could sit and have tea. Richard refused to come with me. I'll never forgive him for that! Geoffrey sent a chauffeur-driven car to take Biddy and me to his place. It was a little terrace house in Norwood, a south-western London suburb. Geoffrey's sister was sweet but very shy. The tea was lovely. There were delicious home-made scones, cakes and sandwiches.

After tea Geoffrey asked if I would like to see his collection of photographs of me. On the door of the room was a wonderful silver plaque on which was engraved 'The

June Bronhill Room'. I fell about laughing. It was very rude of me, but I couldn't help it. 'Oh, Geoffrey,' I said, 'you've got to be joking. This is hysterical!' We opened the door and inside the walls were completely covered with photographs of me in my various roles. They were not just ten-by-eight inch prints, but fifteen-by-twelves, and all in silver frames. It was wonderful but, to me, hysterically funny. I couldn't believe that anybody could go to such extremes. Then Geoffrey brought out his photograph albums. He'd gone through the files in newspaper offices and had copies made of every newspaper photograph ever taken of me. I was bowled over by it all, but I couldn't wait to get out of the house. I found the whole thing claustrophobic.

We continued with the 'in-between-matinee' meals from Fortnum and Masons until one Saturday, when an extraordinary thing happened. In the morning there had been a burst water-main not far from the theatre. Our safety curtain was hydraulic and relied on the water from this main. It took the staff ages to get the curtain up by hand and consequently we were an hour late going up, which meant that we were an hour late coming down. I left word at the stage-door that I couldn't see anybody in between shows because I had about fifteen minutes to change and make-up for my first scene. Suddenly there was a banging on my dressing-room door and I asked who it was.

'It's Geoffrey.'

'Geoffrey, I left a message at the door. I can't possibly see anyone because we were so late going up.'

'All right, if you don't want to see me, this is the last time you'll ever see me.' He walked in and threw the package containing my evening meal at me.

'Geoffrey, it's just that we were an hour late going up because of the burst water-main.'

'I don't want any excuses. That's it!'

And he walked out of my life. I thought he'd just got a bit huffy, that he'd come back, but that was it. I never saw or heard of Geoffrey Pretious from that day to this. I did miss the food, though, and I dread to think what happened to the June Bronhill Room!

When we were doing *The Merry Widow* at the Coliseum in 1958, the stage-door pub was the Lemon Tree, a smashing pub run by Ben and Helen Bromnick. Helen and Ben are a divine couple, absolutely marvellous, the perfect people to run a stage-door pub. Ben had been a jazz musician many years before and understood the business completely. They had a lovely daughter called Hazel and she became completely enraptured by me. She thought I was the best thing since sliced bread. Hazel in those days was my number one fan, apart from Geoffrey Pretious. She was wonderful. Over the years Hazel has become a good friend, and is one of my best friends to this day. She understands completely that I rarely write, that I always forget her birthday. She always remembers mine. The poor love has really been through the mill over the years with an unhappy marriage and other worries. But whenever I'm back in London, Hazel and I have tremendous fun together. Hazel has written some lovely poems, rather of the vein of Rod McKuen, and lyrics to some songs. Before Hazel really got to know me, she would come into the dressing-room and just stand. She wouldn't say anything. I'd ask, 'Did you enjoy it?'

She'd say, 'Yes.'

'Anything in particular you enjoyed?'

'Oh, no—I liked your clothes.'

That turned into our joke eventually. The minute she walked in I'd say, 'Did you like my clothes?' and Hazel would say, 'Yes. You were all right, too.'

When I was doing *The Merry Widow* at Sadler's Wells I suddenly became aware of a woman sitting in the front row. She was there for almost every performance. She scarcely ever took her eyes off me but never came backstage to meet me. It was not until I was doing *Lucia di Lammermoor* at Covent Garden that I met her. She was sitting in the front row again, next to a wonderful woman who was a real Sadler's Wells devotee. She came to everything at the Wells. After the performance, they both came backstage to see me. The woman I'd seen so often at Sadler's Wells was introduced as Peggy Meek. She had an extraordinary stammer and nervous tic in her face. Slowly she told me that she had been a great admirer of Lily Elsie and had seen her playing *The Merry Widow* when she was a child. She told me she thought no one could be as good as Lily Elsie in the title role and when Sadler's Wells started performing the *Widow*, she had refused to see it. In the end, she had given in to her friends and was thrilled because she absolutely loved it. Now she was a great fan of mine. From that moment on, every time Peggy (or Miss Meek, as I called her then) came to the theatre, she came backstage to see me. She was sweet. She never intruded.

About a year after I first met her, she gave me a present, an absolutely exquisite Georgian diamond bow brooch. As I had done with Geoffrey Pretious, I said, 'No, really Miss Meek, I cannot accept it.' She said, 'I'd love you to have it.' And to give her the happiness (and to give me the happiness as well, I suppose) I accepted it. That was the first of many presents that Peggy gave me. I didn't really get to know her properly until I was doing *Robert and Elizabeth*. All I knew about her was that she lived in a bed-sitting room in St Johns Wood and that she liked her little scotch (because I always had drinks in the dressing-room).

One night, Peggy and I were left in the dressing-room together with Richard, my husband. She said to us, 'I do hope you don't feel sorry for me in any way. I have had a wonderful life.' Then she promptly proceeded to tell us about her father who had been a High Court judge and a very wealthy man. When her parents had died, their money went to Peggy and her sister Phoebe. They each had £100,000, and this was in the late 1920s. While Phoebe was the good one of the family, Peggy was the devil and a great gambler. She was part of quite a famous set, the Lonsdale Group, known for their gambling and high living. They used to charter planes, fly over to Le Touquet and gamble the night away, then fly home again. When Peggy came into her inheritance, she gambled her lot away within ten years. She then became a house player, playing for the house at Crockfords, one of the top gambling establishments in London at that time.

She told us all about her wonderful love affairs. Her biggest affair was with a man who, unfortunately, was married. Obviously nothing was ever going to come of it, but she worshipped him so much that she wouldn't dream of marrying somebody else. She said there was no possibility of a divorce. She told me a lovely story of how she and her lover were in a very famous hotel in Jermyn Street where people would take a suite for the afternoon or the evening, have their passionate moments and then have dinner served. It was all terribly elegant and the 'in' thing to do, if you were wealthy or had a wealthy lover. One bitterly cold day, she and her lover had had a marvellous love-making afternoon, with a fire blazing in the fireplace. Afterwards she expected him to say marvellous things about how wonderful it was; instead of which he just leant across, poured himself a scotch and lit a cigarette. Peggy said, 'I was so fffucking fffurious with him! I grabbed the scotch out of his hands and I threw it on the fffire. I nearly set the whole fffucking place alight!' These words coming from Peggy, with her beautifully cultured voice, seemed terribly funny!

After she had explained about her background, I realised that she was very lonely; she had few relatives and they didn't seem to be interested in her. She said that when she visited them, the first thing the children would say was, 'What have you got for me? What presents have you brought me?' She said, 'I don't like that sort of thing in children.' I asked her one Saturday if she'd like to spend Sunday with us and she said she'd be thrilled. On the dot of 12.30 a taxi pulled up outside our mews house in Knightsbridge and Peggy got out, laden with bottles of scotch, gin and brandy, chocolates for Biddy. From that moment she became one of the family. Not because of what she had brought, I hasten to add — we loved her because she was such a gem of a person. Every Sunday Peg would arrive with a bottle of gin, scotch and something for Biddy, so eventually I said, 'Peg, we don't need these things.'

'All right. You tell me what you want and I'll bring whatever you're running short of.' She discovered that Richard smoked Dunhill cigarettes so every week without fail there would be 200 Dunhills for Richie and at least one bottle of something. I had to clamp down on the chocolates for Biddy because we didn't like her eating too many sweets.

One Sunday Peggy arrived with a bottle of everything, chocolates and beautiful Swiss cotton handkerchiefs for me – handrolled and monogrammed – and not a cigarette for Richard. She said, 'Richard, I'm v-very sorry. I haven't g-got your Dunhills. I went to the t-tobacconists yesterday and I said, "I w-w-w; I w-w-want two h-h-h" and I knew I w-wasn't going to g-get it out so I said, "Oh, f-fuck," and walked out!' What a wonderful character she was, a wonderful person. Richard, Biddy and I became quite devoted to her and we spent many happy times together.

When I went away on holiday in 1972, Peggy stayed at my place because I was worried about her. She hadn't been very well, so I had my friend Marje stay there as well to keep an eye on her. I phoned home one morning and asked if I could speak to Peggy. Marje said, 'I'm very worried about her. I found her out of her bed last night on the floor.' When I spoke to Peggy myself her speech was very slurred. I asked Marje if there was any possibility that Peg had any booze stashed away anywhere.

'No way. She had a drink last night but that was all.'

I said, 'I'm a bit worried. She sounds exactly like my father did the night before he had his stroke.' So I rang my doctor in London, Mr McLellan, and asked if he could go over and see her. He phoned me back later and said he was very concerned about her. He had arranged for Peggy to be admitted to an excellent private hospital that afternoon.

I dashed up to London and saw Peggy for the last time

that night. She woke up in the middle of the night, asked the nurse for a cup of tea, had a massive stroke and died. I handled all the funeral arrangements and it really tore me apart. I shall always remember Peggy. She was a dear, and faithful friend, and a generous, warm and loving person.

In the latter part of my life in London, I met another fan called Marjorie Roscoe. Marje also writes me letters, sends me cards and presents and never gets anything in return. I really am very ashamed of myself!

Sometimes in London Marjorie and Hazel used to come visiting at the same time. They were vying for my every word and every look, and it really was very funny for me. It was quite a business getting them out of the house because they wouldn't go together. Each one would try to out-stay the other, until in the end I'd just have to say, 'Sorry girls, I've got to go to bed, so please, off you go. I love you both but cheerio!'

Marje saved all her pennies to come to Australia to visit me when there was no sign of my going back to England. When she was here she said she wanted to see Broken Hill and Adelaide. So we caught the train from Sydney to Broken Hill. The Indian Pacific is a marvellous train. It leaves Sydney about 3.30 p.m. and arrives in Broken Hill about 8.30 a.m. Marje loved the journey through the Blue Mountains. After dinner somebody came up to me and said, 'You are June Bronhill, aren't you?' I said yes, then they asked me if I would sing something. So I sang, unaccompanied, 'Scarborough Fair' and everyone applauded. One man said to me, 'Excuse me, do you sing with a piano?'

'I have been known to. Why?'

'In the lounge next to this there's a piano.'

So we went in there and I gave something like an hour's recital while he accompanied me on the piano. The lounges filled up with travellers enjoying the free concert. I was halfway through a song when suddenly the pianist stopped and said, 'I do hope you'll forgive me, but I've only just realised who you are. You're June Bronhill, aren't you?'

'Yes, I am.'

'How can you ever forgive me?'

'It doesn't matter at all, but tell me about yourself—you're such a marvellous accompanist. You've been here for nearly an hour with me singing away. I tell you what key I want and boom! you play it. You're quite incredible—you are obviously a professional accompanist.' •

'I was one of the main accompanists with the BBC Light Music Department for many years.'

So all those umpteen years ago in London he had probably accompanied me somewhere along the line. And I didn't even have the common courtesy to write down his name, but we did have a great night, all of us, on that train.

Marje loved Broken Hill and took lots of photographs, including one of me outside the house where I was born and grew up and one by Bronhill Street, which was named after me!

I have called this chapter 'My Adoring Public', but of course there have been times when the word 'adoring' obviously has to be used tongue in cheek, or even not used at all! Many times people have got my name wrong, or forgotten it altogether, or confused me with Joan Sutherland. This is something I find amazing, because we're so unalike physically. Joan is tall, I am short. Joan has red hair, I have blonde hair.

One day, when I was in a taxi, the driver kept looking at me, turning his head to look at me, turn back, turn again. In the end it was too much for him and he asked, 'Are you Joan or June?'

'I'm June. Joan's the tall one, I'm the little one.'

'Gets a bit confusing at times,' he said.

It's all very well people confusing your name with somebody else's but when they don't even remember your name it's worse. For example, I was autographing some records in a store in Sydney and I was being interviewed. The girl who was my understudy at the time, Maureen Howard, who is a wonderful performer in her own right, with a beautiful voice, had come along with me. She was suddenly aware of two old biddies that came up and stood next to her. They listened for a while, then one turned to the other and said, 'Who's that?'

The other one said, 'Oh, you know, it's that one who came back.'

I was doing a personal appearance at a shopping centre. I'd had an interview and told various anecdotes about my life. When I'd left the platform a woman came up to me and said, 'You're not June.'

I said, 'Oh, yes, I am, I really am.'

'Oh no, you're not. You're not. June Bronhill's a lot taller than you.'

'No, it's not that at all. A lot of people see me on stage and think that I'm a lot taller.'

'Oh no. You can't fool me. I know what June Bronhill looks like—she's really quite tall, and she's not as fat as you, in any case.'

I could not convince this woman that I was really June Bronhill.

'You're not June, you're definitely not June Bronhill,' she kept muttering.

There is the other side of the story. My dear friend Freddie was in a cocktail bar one evening. A woman came in who looked a little like me. She told the assembled company that she'd been on the *QE2* and had really fooled everybody, including the captain, and had been invited to the captain's cocktail party by telling them that she was June Bronhill. And Freddie didn't say a word. Everbody, of course, knew that he knew me but they didn't say a word and were giving him sidelong glances. Then he had to leave. He said goodbye to everybody and said to the woman, 'Oh, by the way, I happen to know June Bronhill very well—I manage her. She'll be fascinated by this story.'

I don't think she ever imitated me again!

But the public, on the whole, are divine. No matter where I go, people stop me and talk to me. They say they've seen me in one of my shows, *The Merry Widow*, *The Sound of Music*, or in the Australian version of *Are You Being Served?*. It's lovely for them to be able to stop me and have a chat.

Once when Biddy was about twelve and a half, she came over from New Zealand to spend the school holidays with me and we went shopping in David Jones. Lots of people were stopping and looking at me, then coming up and saying, 'Are you who I think you are? Are you June?' And they'd say, 'Oh, we've seen you on television,' and they'd ask me all sorts of questions which I'd answer. I'd pass the time of day with them.

Biddy, after a number of people had stopped and talked to me, said, 'Mummy, are you famous?'

'I suppose I am,' I said. 'I'm very well known because I do lots of television and concerts, and I've also done lots of big productions on stage.'

'What about all these people who stop and talk to you? Doesn't that worry you?'

'Not in the least, darling. These are the people that make my life,' I said. 'When they stop wanting to talk to me, that's when I'll get worried. These people are the most important people to me, apart from you, because without the public I would be nothing.'

Index

208

211

213

215